PENGUIN BOOKS

Understanding Offices

Joanna Eley graduated in Politics, Philosophy and Economics from Oxford before studying architecture at the University of Pennsylvania and at the Bartlett in London University. She works independently, and within teams created by others, and has twenty years of experience in architectural design, consultancy and technical writing. She is interested in how buildings are designed, produced and used. A constant theme in all her work is clarifying how buildings serve their users and are understood by individuals and organizations. She is active in theoretical research, practical consultancy and live building projects, in order to continually refresh and expand her understanding of the real world of buildings and their users. She is co-author of the book *Architects and Their Practices*, which describes the challenge architects face in playing their role in the next century. She has strong ties with the Lake District, but lives in London with her husband and three almost adult children.

Alexi Ferster Marmot trained as an architect in Sydney, before moving to Berkeley, California, to study urban design, and city and regional planning, and to attain her Ph.D. On moving to London she joined Nathaniel Lichfield and Partners, and taught at the Bartlett School, before being appointed as a director at DEGW. She established Alexi Marmot Associates, AMA, in 1990 to advise organizations on the best use of their buildings. She remains intrigued by the connection between people, institutions and their buildings, constantly seeking new ways to document how people use space and react to their environment, and to use that knowledge to make buildings efficient, effective and popular. She is particularly concerned with the impact of teleworking on offices, homes and urban life. She maintains academic and research links with several universities, and is now completing a study of the health effects of the physical environment. She is married and has three children.

Joanna Eley and Alexi Marmot

Understanding Offices

What every manager needs to know about office buildings

Penguin Books

PENGUIN BOOKS

Published by the Penguin Group
Penguin Books Ltd, 27 Wrights Lane, London w8 5tz, England
Penguin Books USA Inc., 375 Hudson Street, New York, New York 10014, USA
Penguin Books Australia Ltd, Ringwood, Victoria, Australia
Penguin Books Canada Ltd, 10 Alcorn Avenue, Toronto, Ontario, Canada m4v 3b2
Penguin Books (NZ) Ltd, 182–190 Wairau Road, Auckland 10, New Zealand

Penguin Books Ltd, Registered Offices: Harmondsworth, Middlesex, England

First published 1995
10 9 8 7 6 5 4 3 2 1

Filmset by Datix International Limited, Bungay, Suffolk
Printed in England by Clays Ltd, St Ives plc
Set in 9/11 pt Monophoto Times

Contents

Introduction

'I hope it's my copy of *Understanding Offices*!'

> 'The flex-firm concept does not imply structurelessness; it does suggest that a company, in being reborn, may cease to be a mule and turn into a team consisting of a tiger, a school of piranhas, a mini-mule or two, and who knows, maybe even a swarm of information-sucking bees. The image underlines the point. The business of tomorrow may embody many different formats within a single frame. It may function as a kind of Noah's Ark.'
>
> A. Toffler, *Powershift*

So where are the instructions for building and sailing Toffler's Ark?

You have attended the conferences and learned what the new business looks like; your organization *is* on the right track to meet the challenges of the twenty-first century; you *have* identified the opportunities and made the changes.

But do you know what sort of building you should be in, and how to use and manage it when you've got it? Do you know whether it will be an office building or something else altogether? Will each office worker get more or less space in future? Will open plan and air-conditioning fall out of favour, as people return to cellular offices and openable windows? Will office buildings fill with leisure and family-support facilities, so that people can spend all their waking hours there, or will they become clubs for an occasional visit?

Management books abound, describing how to lead, how to make one-minute decisions, how to manage difficult people, how to recognize – or reorganize into – a shamrock or a doughnut organization, how to thrive on chaos. Not many of them describe WHERE all this takes place – the physical realities as opposed to the management attitudes and structures that support the business. Material written about buildings is directed either at facilities managers, concerned with running buildings, now establishing themselves as a 'profession', or at the inward-looking world of designers, property agents and builders.

Office workers are increasingly important in the running of the economy. They make up half of all those in active work. Their importance will increase as many other jobs decline absolutely in advanced economies. In the UK alone there are now over 10 million office workers. They work in about 200 million square metres (2,000 million square feet) gross of office space, representing about £120 billion of capital investment. Just to heat, clean, manage and insure this space annually costs in the order of £10 billion. There is a multitude of office buildings, large and small, old and new, in urban and out-of-town locations, in single- and multi-occupancy, purpose-built and converted from other uses. Some office work takes place in specialized buildings, such as hospitals, schools, theatres, museums, airports, factories, warehouses and shops. All these places are where white-collar workers spend much of their time and find at least part of their identity. The many organizations using the buildings constantly adapt and change them to suit their evolving needs or build new ones if nothing already available will do. This book has been written to help managers in all these organizations to understand their office space. This will make it easier for them to get the best out of their buildings, to use the precious, scarce resource of built space efficiently and to create a good-quality environment in which their staff can work effectively. The knowledge and skills required to get the best out of office buildings can be applied to any other building type where office activities are to be housed. At the same time a question must also be asked: what is the future need for the offices likely to be?

The office of the future or the future of the office?

> 'The business of the future may be run by executives who are scarcely ever in each other's physical presence. It will not even have an address or a central office – only the equivalent of a telephone number. For its files and records will be space rented in the memory units of computers that could be located anywhere on Earth ... vast memory banks beneath the Arizona desert ... or wherever land is cheap and useless for any other purpose.'
>
> Arthur C. Clarke, *Profiles of the Future*

A new generation of changed organizational patterns and social consequences is upon us. We have to re-examine what we need offices for, what we can justify in their name. If information handling is carried out more efficiently by dispersed groups networked to powerful computers, why should we need offices? If we can stop them guzzling so much energy, will we still be able to afford offices? Can we make sure that they are located where they can be reached without a two-hour journey in overcrowded conditions? Will people still want to come to office buildings? Will future offices have to take a 'green agenda' into account? Will there actually be office buildings in the future?

Offices have flowered as a building form, and a social structure, for a fairly short, intense period. They seem to have permeated totally our understanding of the world of work. But they could be a short-lived phenomenon, a transitional stage in man's economic evolution. Agriculture had its buildings – barns, byres, warehouses, transport depots. Then, for manufacturing, factories and power stations were invented. The 'new industrial state' needed office buildings, and they were built by the thousand, ripping the factories and warehouses out of urban centres and creating the new image of the city in the twentieth century. Now we are moving to a new phase in which the buildings that will be needed are unknown, a phase of information manipulation that will require networks of wires and waves linking networks of buildings that may not be like any we have now. What is there about office buildings that could encourage them to disappear? What is there that will keep them alive and well and living in the future? The number of people working in offices has grown throughout this century, as shown on p. xii. From now on the number of people needing to work in offices may start to decline.

A rich variety of uses is being found for redundant churches. Their regular use has declined, and congregations have dwindled. What used to be daily attendance fell to once weekly then, for many, to the main festivals of the Church year or not at all. Minority religions with small but dedicated groups of followers, scattered across the country, each pursuing an individual approach, have flourished and located in various building types. Redundant churches have been adapted to emerge as theatres, gymnasiums, community halls, video studios and flats. Is this a pattern that can dimly be seen to have parallels in the office world? Will our present office buildings be redundant in the next century, reused for other activities, as the churches are today, while office activities are scattered elsewhere? The vision painted by Clarke thirty years ago, which he placed a century into the future, around 2060, is already easy to picture given current equipment – far easier than he anticipated.

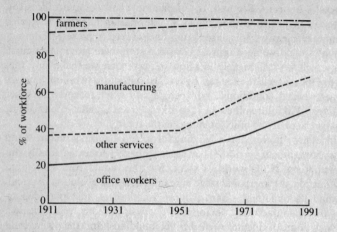

Figure 0   Increase in office workforce, 1900–2000.

Source: 1911–71 from G. Routh, *Occupation and Pay in Great Britain 1906–1979*, Macmillan, London, 1980, p. 11; 1991 data from OPCS, *1991 Census Report for Great Britain, Part 2*, HMSO, London, 1993, table 74.

Still, it is hard to imagine administration, government, organizational management being carried out entirely through computer networks between remote individuals without anything like offices, places where people come together to work, resembling in essentials the offices we know today. The routines involved in governing large groups of people, supplying them with the goods and services they need for survival or demand for enjoyment, require cooperation. Only if the entire population shrank to tiny numbers, and had the support of relatively indestructible machinery, could sophisticated societies manage with significantly fewer office-type activities.

It is in order to enhance the necessary cooperation that offices will continue to exist. People need to be trained to enable them to work together effectively. Some of this training will take place in offices. Corporate culture needs to be transmitted to new recruits. Home video training, corporate conferences or computer courseware will not achieve this unaided. It is when they are physically together that people can best get to know each other, understand each other's skills and weaknesses, learn by example, find those people with whom they work best and discover in what type of work they themselves excel. Once trained, socialized into cooperation, teamwork or individual work, many people can be liberated to work in a wide variety of locations, some of which will be offices. Only a few of those so liberated will actually want to take up the freedom. Others will need the companionship and constancy of an office routine, for some or all of the time.

Though offices will continue to be needed, it will be for a different working population. At present 50 per cent of the total UK workforce is in office-based white-collar jobs. The full extent to which this percentage will change can only be guessed. The overall numbers are likely to increase – office-based work still has some sources of growth, even though most other sectors of the economy are likely to stagnate or decline. Despite this, the need for space in office building will decline as a result of a drive for economy and the fact that the office workforce spends less time in offices. Already there are some users who occupy an office for very few of the available hours. The building is always present, every hour of every day of its long life. Office workers spend a very small proportion of that time there. They are away from the building because of weekends, leave and sickness, because the remaining working days use only eight of the available twenty-four hours and because office hours are spent elsewhere for meetings, training or work in other locations. In some cases workers may spend as little as 5 per cent of the available hours in their office building. This sounds ridiculous, but in the case of anyone who is habitually out of the office for an average three and a half days per week, and takes his or her full complement of annual leave, that is what is happening. These people are not freaks; many jobs involve this sort of work pattern, from those of salesmen to senior managers, from two-day-a-week academics to expensive management consultants. How far the provision of buildings for such a work pattern can be justified is one of the issues that must be addressed.

The percentage of available time spent in offices by some people is much higher than this, but it is declining. According to present trends, overall the proportion of a white-collar person's working life spent in an office will decline, even in the case of those people whose jobs keep them at their office desk all of every working day. The length of a person's working life has been shrinking, absolutely and relatively. The average length of life is increasing, but young people are in education for longer, so they start working life later, and retirement age is getting younger. The number of days of annual holiday to which people are entitled has expanded, with the two-day weekend replacing the single day or one and a half days, the increased number of public holidays and the longer personal holiday allowances being offered by many organizations. The length of the working day has also been gradually reduced. If these trends continue, offices may change, as they will provide for a different amount of an individual's time and perhaps a different aspect of their identity. These trends are of great importance to women who make up the office workforce. There have always been large numbers of women in the most lowly clerical capacity. Many once worked only while young and childless. More women these days continue to work after starting a family. Their requirements are for shorter journeys to work and part-time work or job-sharing that allows them to combine work with child care. Office technology liberates location, allowing offices in or near their homes to function as well as central ones.

Places where people can come together and marshal, exchange and use information will still be needed, even for a smaller workforce, which spends fewer hours per year in office buildings. What will these buildings be like? There are various signs of problems with the office buildings we know: dislike of air-conditioning, risk from bombs, the need for huge transport infrastructures to support them. Suggestions for alternatives include neighbourhood offices and business/office parks. Some suggestions in chapter 1 are in vogue with those who focus on the mobile workforce. The *club*, the relaxed lounge with refreshments and interesting discussions with colleagues, is the favourite image.

In fact, the old Lloyd's Coffee House in the City of London, the birthplace of the huge insurance offices, is back in favour. Such buildings would be used by a much larger number of people than current office buildings accommodate because so many would be away at any one time. This is one way of improving the use made of a building. Individuals would be away from the office more, allowing them to live their personal lives, more integrated with their working lives, elsewhere. Another image is the *work palace*, a building with a range of excellent and exclusive facilities so that staff could spend the whole day there, using the office to support personal life, leisure, entertainment and family care – making use of crèches or even granny-care units. This would also help to make better use of the building as a whole, even while the hours spent on paid work are reduced. Another possibility is the *technoemporium*, a building that acts as a repository of electronic gadgets, where desks groan under ever more exotic equipment. Such offices could be much smaller, used in short, sharp bursts when large, expensive, non-portable equipment is required. There would be shelves in the stockroom dispensing the latest pocket-sized gizmo to use away from the office. This is another way to help maintain a good level of use of a building. All of these are, of course, caricatures – recognizable ones, bits of which exist already. A patchwork is the most likely outcome, with different emphases on these various outcomes, some of which could be brought together in the mix that works best for each organization, in buildings that are 'intelligent' or 'forgiving' enough to accommodate them in changing proportions over time, without too much strain. The emphasis will always be on how to make good use of a building, which is an expensive resource, to serve more people for longer and to accommodate activities that cannot easily take place elsewhere.

Location, location and location

The three most important factors ('location, location and location') that estate agents have told us for years matter most when selecting office buildings or sites to develop, have meant, until now, that the desirable locations are the ones that other people have already chosen. As a result they are densely developed and expensive and often entail a tedious and stressful journey from where most people live. Such locations are also vulnerable to disruption on a massive scale – when transport systems break down through strikes or technical failure, or when terrorists decide to hit. The simple principle 'Don't put all your eggs in one basket' has an important place in planning office accommodation, if in no other way than to alert companies to the need for disaster planning.

Location and transport are intimately linked, and there are real opportunities for major energy savings by reducing or eliminating the journey to work. This saving is not reaped directly by the organization. If private-car commuting is the predominant mode of travel, then locating an office to which people can walk, bike or take a local bus will make enormous energy savings. This fact is behind some of the changes in office-work patterns that have taken place in the USA. For example, in Los Angeles, to reduce the energy consumption of government office organizations, several are reducing the number of commuter journeys made by encouraging some staff to work at home for one or two days a week. Local offices have been developed where people can go to work if they prefer not to work in their own homes. The location equation is changing to help reduce national levels of energy consumption and pollution.

The new way of working described in chapter 1, the freedom from dependence on location, has been fairly well explored in the national and the technical press, from the point of view of an individual office worker. There are fewer people willing to stand up and be counted when it comes to describing what this will really mean for the locations of the office buildings of the future. Will they migrate to residential neighbourhoods or to motorway intersections? Will the new locations be served by public transport? If people can work anywhere, will they insist on working in a convenient place? If so, convenient for what? Home or urban facilities? Will management seek cheaper locations and forgo the face-to-face opportunities of densely packed city centres? All these forces seem to be having a small effect here and there: nothing definite enough to allow a decisive judgement to be pronounced that change is gathering momentum and city centres will not be office locations in the future, yet not so insignificant that it would be safe to say the opposite. The forces that have centralized large parts of the office-working population in major cities, in densely developed locations, acted over many decades. A slow reversal seems to be taking place. What could speed things up would be a change in the amount of pressure applied to organizations to act in environmentally responsible ways, as in California, where it is already happening. It may become greatly intensified. Large costs associated with transporting big populations in individual cars can be measured and passed on to offending organizations. Alternatively, more office staff may vote with their feet, or their wheels, and accept only convenient jobs – though recessions cast a slight sense of fantasy over that scenario.

It could go either way

A hundred years from now, though offices may be different, many office buildings that exist now will still be here. They will have to be made as sustainable as possible in terms of the design of upgrades, the control of energy costs and the tailoring of all consumable and management practices to a green agenda as well as to immediate business objectives.

That is, if people have not abandoned them. Cheap overseas labour, fewer regulations concerning working conditions and the possibility of instantaneous information transfer make offshore office activities a potentially attractive opportunity. Just as manufacturing has moved to developing countries, large parts of the office work currently carried out in attractive offices, by organizations managed by readers of this book, could be exported. This would leave many office buildings in the developed world redundant. Only a few would be needed as offices. The rest would be converted, probably to housing or leisure facilities, or pulled down or, most disastrously and perhaps most likely, allowed to rot where they stand.

Immediate concerns must take precedence over imaginary scenarios. There are plenty of opportunities at the moment to improve the office building, new or old, and make it a better place.

Why does the building matter?

The office building is the Ark in which most business still sails. Good managers understand their building. They excel if their office building supports the way they want their firm to function, if it helps people to communicate, if it gives customers the right image. They know that they have a competitive advantage if their building performs better than the norm through efficient design and space management. They seek to make the most of their property assets to support their core business.

Yet senior managers are often in the dark about their buildings. They are responsible for the mission statement for a business, but often they are not in close contact with the people whose job it is to see that a building, with its equipment and furnishing, properly supports the business to achieve this mission. Property directors are appointed in only a small percentage of companies. The director responsible for property is most likely to be a finance director. But finance directors have more important things to worry about than buildings, don't they? Even property directors are more likely to be expert in the financial side of property deals than in understanding what makes the property that they occupy useful and attractive, or inhibiting and unpleasant, for their organization.

'Office' turns out, if you look at the dictionary, to be an overworked word. What does the word conjure up for you? Is your office the organization to which you belong in your work role? Or is it the building where you work, or perhaps your own little room in that building, or maybe the one at home where you retreat on Sunday afternoons? All these meanings, and a great many more, are perfectly valid as far as the dictionary is concerned. The word is used to refer to a role, the job that a person has in an 'official' capacity. It is attached to the place where 'clerkly' activities are carried out, an office building. The place where specific activities are carred out in an organization, such as the 'booking office' in a railway station, or whole organizations that have a particular role, such as the Post Office', have incorporated the word in their titles, implying both a role and an activity. 'Office' is also used to mean all the people within an organization, and people from many organizations are sometimes referred to collectively as 'office' workers. Most of the time in this book we use the word 'office' to mean 'office building', though when discussing enclosed personal 'offices' it is also used to refer to rooms. Problems arise in discussing the fragmentation of the 'office', when the dissolution of the group carrying out the work is the topic, but we have done our best to make the various meanings clear as they shift and merge.

This book is about productive buildings for leading-edge organizations. We admire unreservedly office buildings of breathtaking architecture and rich interior design. But aesthetic concerns are the focus of books for the design community. We adopt the view that office buildings can be analysed rationally and sensible decisions can be taken if managers only know the right questions. This book helps them formulate those questions.

We have not prepared an exhaustive academic treatise on office design. This book seeks to demystify a technical subject for the benefit of people whose specialist skills lie in other fields but for whom this information is important. Many good ideas we have come across, those of clients and colleagues from all over the world, have been pressed into service. We have quoted comments from the thousands of individuals whom we have observed, or interviewed while developing plans for their office space, using our many techniques to understand their real needs. Clients in large and small organizations, public and private, in the UK and elsewhere, in lavish or humble premises, have provided us with insights and much of the material upon which this book is based. Rather than scatter footnotes throughout the book on the origin of each thought, we have collected key references to important reading material in a list at the end. No one should underestimate the contribution that these other writers and practitioners have made to our work. What we have made of their ideas is our own responsibility.

No attempt is made to make a space-planning expert out of every reader. The aim is to give insights about office buildings to managers, even those who expect to leave building planning and management to others. Better decisions can be made if managers understand generic information about buildings and their fittings. They can then help to choose and use buildings that will serve the company mission well. Many issues are discussed in the context of existing premises occupied by existing organizations. Most people are in this situation most of the time. Yet it is at the time of a move that everyone wants the answers to many of the questions addressed here. Sometimes this is a good time to get people's attention and enable resources to be devoted to seeking answers and understanding their implication. Often it is not. At the moment of a move everyone concerned has too many different agendas, too little time to think straight and too much to do. A move is threatening, and many people may find it hard to make constructive contributions. If some of the ideas discussed in this book can be considered in the relative calm of an existing building, the organization will be better equipped for a future move, should it arise, as well as getting more out of its current situation. None the less, if a move is happening willy-nilly, this book can be used to clarify potential solutions in an as yet unselected building, to aid participation in briefing and making decisions about a new building or to help assess several existing buildings in order to make a suitable choice.

New ways of working are making news. Their consequences for making best use of a building, in space and time, are looked at in chapter 1. But these apply only to some businesses all of the time, even if they may eventually apply to all businesses some of the time. In all circumstances buildings need to be understood if they are to serve their users well. Fundamental information about the size, efficiency and other aspects of a building that affect its utility is reviewed in chapter 2. Space standards and the dichotomy of the desire for enclosed offices versus the benefits and realities of open space planning are covered in chapters 3 and 4. Chapter 5 considers furniture and lighting, chapter 6 discusses the mysterious issues of sick-building syndrome and comfort. Space that does not contain desks and enclosed offices – amenity areas, both required and optional – are discussed in chapter 7. Chapter 8 looks at the future and considers developments in information technology and whether office buildings, as we know them, can be sustainable and responsible in years to come. An office move, the moment to reap the benefits of the material discussed in earlier chapters, is the subject of the final chapter.

1 Location-free Work

'Nowadays he prefers to phone in his performance.'

> **Q: When is an office not an office?**
> A: When it's 'hot', virtual, a twisted pair or a gentleman's club.

This answer is directed at organizations with:
- a large proportion of office space empty much of the time
- salesmen who should be with their customers, telesales people
- creative writers, software writers, journalists, copy-editors who work odd hours in odd places
- consultants or auditors who work on client premises
- inspectors who must make visits
- sophisticated and widely distributed communications technology
- a need to keep or attract valuable staff by allowing them to choose to work from home for at least some of the time
- other people for whom new ways of working are of growing relevance.

Your office is where YOU are

We acclimatized to the notion that offices are places where many people are gathered together to work on paper-related tasks and have forgot the earlier examples of small-scale or individual places of work. For a while. Now that image is being challenged.

Much has been written about the design of offices. Fortunes have been made and lost on the property market by creating and selling buildings intended for office occupation. At the same time, unnoticed by the majority but accepted as unremarkable by those concerned, some types of white-collar office workers have not actually worked much in office buildings; their work has been where they are. Her Majesty's Inspectors, engaged in planning inquiries, hold their inquiries in locations related to the problem. Their 'office' work – setting up inquiry dates, writing reports – has traditionally been done from home or wherever they find convenient. They do not have an office 'to go back to'. Insurance salesmen may have a filing cabinet in an office somewhere, but their real base is their car or their briefcase.

As communications technology has grown more sophisticated and the kit has shrunk, the possibility of office work outside the office has acquired a glamorous veneer. A design competition in 1980 to provide ideas for the 'office of the future' was won by a submission showing not a building bristling with technology but a briefcase fitted with a computer, a telephone and other electronic marvels, then only embryonic, now commonplace. Advertisers show Transit vans furnished as travelling meeting rooms – office caravans – for those valuable members of organizations who need to be in two or more places at once. Airline seats are sold by TV ads of dynamic, upwardly mobile office people working on their lap-top computers one moment, dining on caviare and champagne the next and sitting in the same seat throughout.

The next step is to make work look like a holiday, the lap-top on the beach, business and pleasure combined as never before. This is a big leap. A new icon represents 'office work'. It is not the office block, that focus of frenetic investment, the concrete-and-glass monument to commerce designed to house an ever-increasing army of office workers. It is an 800-gram battery-powered 'notebook', with at least 36 MB of RAM, that you, a solitary individual, wrap in your bathing towel.

Dependence on the office building as a place has clearly been reduced. The reasons are not far to seek. The development of efficient offices, as we know them now, was much influenced by the development of equipment for communications: the typewriter and the telephone are obvious examples. They helped to bring people together in a single location, to 'glue' them together to exploit the equipment and enhance the value that could be obtained from it. The very same equipment, in its latest versions, is now acting as a powerful 'solvent'. Information at the most sophisticated level, of complex and subtle content, can be carried over vast distances, instantly and cheaply. The developments that in the early 1980s brought different types of office equipment closer together as a result of miniaturization, and increased the processing power of computers, seemed likely to lead to single machines that could do everything (the colour-printing and collating and binding of a document directly transmitted from a computer, for example), to the convergence of different bits of expensive equipment into a single, very clever one.

These developments have indeed come about, resulting in equipment that can virtually perform magic tricks and is still capable of representing 'glue', as did the first telephones or computers, in that it is expensive, has huge capacity and can best be exploited in a place were large groups of people can come together – an office.

At the same time various functions, such as computing, telephoning, faxing and colour copying, are being released in cheap, miniature, portable versions. (So the solvent has been created by another version of the 'glue' technology, packaged and sold in a different way.) The telephone wires that have linked all buildings since they first appeared can be used to transmit data as easily as speech. Now anything that can be rendered into digital signals can be sent anywhere, and reconstituted on arrival, for manipulation on a large, expensive, centralized bit of equipment or, equally easily, on a small, cheap one that lives in the back of the car at the bottom of the suitcase, in the team room at the office or beside the TV at home.

New ways of working

'New ways of working' seem an unlikely topic for much excitement, yet the centrality of this subject must be appreciated. In our culture many measures of value attributed to people are related to their identity at work. This is why the debates about new ways of working, new solutions to the place, the rules, the trappings surrounding work, are of such interest – why a better grasp of any facts, as opposed to fantasies, is important for today's managers.

Responses to new technology in the office embrace a wide spectrum. A variety of new ways of working is practised, to varying degrees, by different organizations. There are companies that do not acknowledge the changes in ways of working that technology has made possible, because, like proverbial ostriches with their heads in the sand, they have not taken notice of them, or because they have seen and rejected them as passing fads of no interest or relevance, or because they believe they cannot afford them. Others have started to challenge the conventions of the office hierarchy of status and rank.

A small but influential number of people are enthusiastically and aggressively adopting changes that challenge the time and place constraints of office work and use the availability of cheap technology to liberate people from location and from the nine-to-five day. These organizations have espoused location-free working to a lesser or greater degree. Two behaviour patterns that are attracting particular attention are 'telecommuting' and 'hot-desking'. Both these concepts have been variously defined, widely publicized and claimed to have great importance – telecommuting because it will be practised by many people, hot-desking because it will save companies space and therefore money. These concepts depend on office work taking place somewhere else than in the office building.

The office: a factory process or a personal service?

An office is assumed to be a well-understood type of place, office work an accepted and normal activity. In reality office work, based in a place called an 'office', is a relatively recent phenomenon. The need and ability to bring a number of people together in one place to work on information, on paper or, now, on computers is familiar to twentieth-century town and city dwellers. It would have baffled a fifteenth-century craftsman, as much as a nineteenth-century factory would have done. The most office-like environment in the fifteenth century would have been a sort of factory, an assembly of monks and scribes seated at writing desks copying books, perhaps with one member of the group sitting at the front, reading an improving text to divert the minds, but not the hands, of the copyists – a bit like 'Music While You Work' provided by the BBC for the factory floor. But the task would have been one of making books, not collecting and manipulating knowledge in the furtherance of a separate business objective. Office work, depending on this collecting, ordering, manipulating and passing on of information, was not a common part of that world. These functions must have been needed for some exceptional organizations – the Vatican, or the Imperial Chinese Army. They would not have been part of everyday life.

About 150 years ago, when these information-based activities had become more commonplace, the notion that 'your office is where you are' would have been a natural one. For example, the management of an estate took place in an 'estate office' on a landlord's main premises, but the manager could and would carry all the necessary information with him to outlying properties and perform the paperwork tasks wherever he needed to be. Again, a member of the gentry wishing to see a lawyer would summon the lawyer to him and see him in his own home, where the necessary business could be transacted, rather than making a trip to the solicitor's 'office'. The architect's office in Dickens's *Dombey and Son*, where projects for clients and training of hopeful new young architects took place, was, in fact, his own home.

As the number of people who were engaged on office work grew, work involving the transmission of ideas and facts, generally on paper, there was increasingly a reason for bringing these people together in one place, an office, where they could share the ever more complicated paper tasks, divided into steps and stages and be managed as a whole unit of 'production'. Technologies to serve these activities were developed that involved capital outlay, and bulky, heavy equipment such as typewriters or complex adding machines. The reasons to go to an office increased. There the tasks could be carried out with maximum efficiency and minimum outlay on the equipment, which could be shared, as required, by all the people in the office. The telephone created a further powerful reason to come together in one place, where communications were at their most intense. Transport systems were developed to bring people from their homes to their offices and became another factor strengthening the concept of working together in offices, paper 'factories'. To distinguish them from the workers in blue overalls in industrial factories, office workers became known as white-collar workers.

Telecommuting

If people need to communicate at all with colleagues, using data links (the 'tele' bit of telecommuting) reduces their need to travel physically, to 'commute' to work. Telecommuting does not always mean working from home, though it is often assumed to. The essential component is the ability to work somewhere other than in an office building but to be connected to it. The 'father' of telecommuting, Jack Nilles in California, predicted ten years ago that many millions of people would be working this way by the year 2000. Since then every crystal-gazing organization has added its mite to the hype, and it would by now be tempting to imagine that soon there will be no need for office buildings at all. The Henley Centre for Forecasting, in late 1993, suggested that 4 per cent of the UK workforce, 1.2 million people, already use their home as an office, at least for part of the time, and Nilles suggests that 4 million are doing it in the US. Organizations are encouraging staff to work from home some of the time, in order, among other reasons, to reduce the pollution caused by the wholesale movement of people on a daily basis from one building to another and back again. Public agencies in

California, for example, have been participating in the California Telecommuting Project since 1985. They want staff to stay away from the office, doing what can be done anywhere if the right equipment is there. British Telecom, and all the data-carrier companies, are striving hard to ensure that the equipment is indeed there by actively marketing equipment to home-based workers. The Ideal Home exhibition in London, demonstrating the most up-to-date and appealing gimmicks for the home, has seen fit to feature the home office as its centrepiece. Providers of home furniture market the home office desk, competing in their efforts with the office-furniture suppliers who also market several versions. Shelves in the DIY section of bookshops groan under the weight of manuals about creating the home office. Newsletters for telecommuters explain how to discover the most useful bits of equipment, publicizing the most recent successful spin-off of a group of employees into home-based independence. Associations of teleworkers aim to ensure that members have the right insurance cover, that work opportunities and teleworkers can be matched. Banks issue new small-business customers with home-based business machines. The focus of interest is that part of the workforce that is able and willing to work in their own homes. The assumption behind much current management literature is that this is a potentially widespread phenomenon.

Charles Handy, in his book *The Empty Raincoat*, says:

> *The new shape of work will centre around small organizations, most of them in the service sector, with a small core of key people and a collection of stringers or portfolio workers in the space around the core ... Software, telecommunications, environmental engineering, health products and services, and specialized education are increasingly the province of the tiny partnership. They are well suited to the portfolio worker, who costs much less if the firm does not have to house him or her.*

No one would be surprised if these portfolio workers turned out to work 'from home' with a personal computer, an answering machine and a fax and fill in their tax returns as self-employed individuals.

When they are not self-employed but still part of the company, these people may represent a problem for their employer. English managers, unlike managers in other European countries, say that they find it harder to conceive of managing efficiently people who are out of sight. Managers seem to be afraid that if the workers are out of sight, the tasks will be out of mind and not be efficiently performed.

> 'Do you not work at home, at least for some of the time?'
> 'Never. Of course, I could do much of my stuff there.'
> 'So why don't you?'
> 'They won't let me.'
> She pointed to the end of the room where, behind two large glass windows, sat the two deputy editors. 'They like to have me where they can see me and shout at me.'
>
> Atlanta journalist talking to Charles Handy (*The Empty Raincoat*)

This is a mythical problem. People willing to work at home or away from the office are usually well able to take on board the need to complete tasks and to perform to a standard, rather than to put in hours. The real barrier may actually reside in the legal responsibility for an employer to see that staff are working in safe, healthy, insurable conditions wherever they may be. As discussed in later chapters, providing suitable furniture, lighting and air quality in an office building is fraught with pitfalls. To do so in the homes of employees presents even more of an obstacle course.

Not all work, and not all homes, are suited to home-based work. Some organizations are seeking solutions where the commute is reduced but may not be eliminated; work takes place near but not at home. From Sweden to Hawaii via the Scottish Highlands, there are experiments with telecottages, neighbourhood work centres. A telecottage is described as:

> a community centre, equipped with modern technology such as computers, fax and photocopiers, where local people can train or work using the resources provided ... A community based workforce is a more committed workforce; this shows an increased motivation and productivity. City based companies are realising this, and more and more work is being tendered out to telecottages, reversing the centralising effects of the industrial revolution.
>
> TeleCottages Wales, supported by the Welsh Development Agency.

There are examples of workforces in unexpected, unconventional, non-office buildings, such as prisoners in an Irish jail handling the claims forms for an insurance company in the USA. One well-known, constantly quoted and much researched organization in the UK, a pioneer of teleworking, is F International, a computer-programming company. It pioneered home-based working in the 1970s, being staffed by a group who preferred, and were able, to do part of their work in their own homes – women with children, with high qualifications and expert skills, who might otherwise have been lost to the labour market. Interestingly, though, this group, once 600 staff with office space sufficient for sixty, has changed somewhat over time. It now has several office buildings; project teams are as likely to be based in the FI offices as on client premises or at home. The difference between this and many other consultancy organizations has diminished. The office building, and the scope it offers their functions, has been found to have a value.

Working from home sounds idyllic if the home is spacious, in a peaceful environment, well equipped. But many people prefer to keep a distance between their home life and their office. Home is less attractive for work if it is too small to provide a permanent place for the computer, or is filled with the noise of wailing two-year-olds or discontented teenagers out of work and into reggae, or cold because keeping the heating on all day is too expensive. There are numerous difficulties to be resolved. Who pays the telephone bill? Do benefits, such as an agreement for the employer to pay a suitable proportion of the heating bill have to be taxed? Who pays insurance, to cover what eventualities?

'I would be quite happy to work from home. I don't particularly like coming into the office because it's particularly uncomfortable – it's very humid and gets very oppressive. It's also very noisy, so you can hear a phone conversation three, four, five desks away and that can be very distracting.'

'If I've got anything difficult to do, I stay at home – there's too many interruptions, it's too noisy in the office.'

'I would kill to have a computer at home . . . and a printer.'

But on the other hand:

'I view my home as somewhere in which the company doesn't intrude.'

'I would not like to work at home, I like to keep home and work separate.'

'I've got everything I need in the office and I've got the people I need in the office. The remoteness of the home situation means I'd miss out on a lot of the informal side of things. I like the discipline.'

Questionnaire responses: management consultants in an office with pooled desks

Will home office furniture have to comply with ergonomic requirements that are enforceable in an office setting? There are different home circumstances, different answers to these questions given by each organization and different individual temperaments, so people, even in a single organization, do not agree. There are strong feelings expressed on both sides of the argument.

Figure 1.1 Going to work – at home.

Unallocated desks

Consultancy organizations, among others, are exploring another parallel avenue, that of 'desk sharing' or 'hot desking', as a way to acknowledge, and thereby exploit, the change in working patterns. With desk sharing, or pooling, someone who has just walked through the office door settles down at any one of the available desks. The term 'hot desking', borrowed from 'hot bunking' on ships, assumes that the desk has just been vacated by a colleague and is reoccupied before the chair has had time to cool down. Desks are dubbed 'touchdowns' when it is assumed that people settle there only briefly, like butterflies flitting in and out of the office. Why even consider such a horrendous idea? Isn't it a thin disguise for squeezing people into unacceptably tight spaces? Who wants to give up the ownership of his of her desk? What lunatic is willing to give up their own DESK? Who can stand sharing? Will any managers be willing to give up their own OFFICES?

Desk sharing may or may not operate at the same time, or for the same individuals, as telecommuting. When one worker is at home, or working on an aeroplane or a train, another one can be using the desk in the office. The convention whereby everyone is allocated a place of their own has been effectively challenged. What is new is that so much management attention is being applied to an alternative. But creating new conventions by overtly undoing the old is much more difficult than simply tolerating some unconventional groups on the fringes of the organization.

Not surprisingly, it is not just fashion that allows these threatening ideas to be considered. The search for an effective change in today's conventions has developed from the realization that, for many types of so-called office work, the last place you would expect to find the worker is in the office. One of the best-known organizations to examine the possibilities in this area is IBM, whose very existence has flourished by developing and exploiting changes in the technology surrounding office work. IBM started its investigations, in the UK, Canada, Japan and Australia, based on the knowledge that its sales force was not supposed to be in the office. Salesmen were meant to be maximizing 'face time' with potential or existing clients. This is better done on a client's premises than in the salesman's own office, the place where other salesmen are working on deals with the client's competitors. An active sales force results in a sea of empty desks, an expensive luxury at £300–£1,000 per square metre.[1] The same holds true for many sales organizations. Other types of people are often out of the office. Consultants, whose task is to get to know well the business of another organization in order to tailor their specific expert knowledge to the needs of that organization, spend part, sometimes most, of their time on its premises.

[1] Metric measurements are generally given throughout this book. It is over twenty years since the building trade in the UK went metric. Ten square feet are approximately equal to 1 square metre, (to be accurate 10.764 sq ft = 1 sq m). This crude conversion of area figures for the purpose of orders of magnitude is easy: just multiply the number of square metres by 10 if you always use square feet. Nothing more is required.

Other examples are inspectors checking that firms are following correctly the rules laid down for them by taxation, health and safety or other employment regulations, who often need to see the organizations actually at work, or journalists away collecting material before crafting it into reports, or researchers out gathering data or interviewing people. All these are among the groups whose work takes them 'out of the office' and may keep them out more than in.

The space–time equation

In well-managed companies the aim is now to make best use of time as well as space in a building. The methods used to observe and document the use of space over time also allow managers to understand in more detail how staff spend their days. This can in itself be very helpful, not only when replanning space.

Managers or staff may 'know' what their general patterns of behaviour are, but little direct thought is usually directed at understanding the way in which people use buildings, so their knowledge is often mythological, only approximating to the truth. Careful documentation of whether and when people use their desks and offices can show startling results. Detailed observation may indicate that for as much as 80 per cent of the working day no use is made of the workplace provided. In effect, a person is in the office on average only one day in the week. While people may be aware that the nature of a job implies that this is likely to be the case, such knowledge is rarely translated into information bearing directly on the use of space.

Tools for looking at desk and space use and deciding ratios have been developed for, and used by, numerous organizations. They involve observers recording use of space or activities that staff are engaged in. Records are made systematically, in a fashion similar to old 'time-and-motion' studies. The outcome is a record of space productivity, or the way whole groups of people make use of space over time. Another source of information is diaries, filled in over a week or more, indicating where people have spent different parts of the working day. The results of these investigations give a graphic representation of where people need to be and what use is being made of office premises.

It is easy to see why giving everyone their own desk may not make economic sense (where these sorts of data emerge). It is less easy to decide how many desks to give between how many people, what the rules should be about who gets priority in their use and how to deal with numerous practical details about sizes of groups, location of

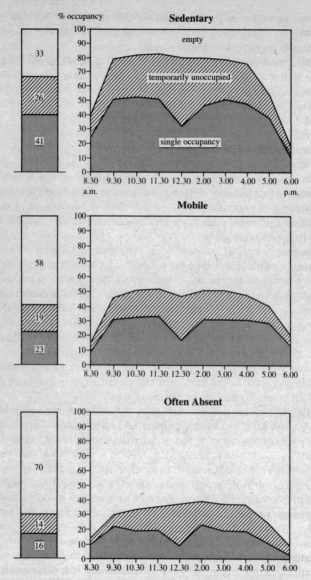

Figure 1.2   How different people use desks over the working day.

Source: Alexi Marmot Associates, space-occupancy studies for various organizations.

personal storage, the nature of equipment needed at the desk and proximity to other office facilities. And what is the significance, if any, of the difference between pooled and shared desks?

What is well-occupied space? Other fields use various rules of thumb. Many airlines, theatres and hotels find that 60 per cent occupancy represents break-even and that 70 per cent is needed for a healthy financial position. Above that figure handsome profits accrue. To have hospital beds available for unexpected and emergency situations, and for orderly change-over of patients, 5 per cent must be empty at any one time. More vacancies increase the cost of health care; fewer mean that life-threatening shortages arise. In an office, if everyone always worked at their desk when not on holiday, or ill, or on courses or training, they would still be using the desk for only 75–85 per cent of the working day, depending on the holiday allowances and opportunity for training provided as part of their job. Those people who are also away from their desk for meetings or work outside the office with clients or travelling, or are at home, may be at their desks for only 10–20 per cent of the working day. So should your office be like a hotel and aim for 70–80 per cent occupancy as a reasonably fully occupied desk pool? Or could you be more like a hospital and aim for 95 per cent?

Work pattern	Typical ratio of desks to people	Percentage desks
Sedentary	1 : 1	100%
Mobile	0.7 : 1 to 0.4 : 1	50% to 70%
Often absent	0.3 : 1 to 0.1 : 1	10% to 30%

Figure 1.3 Planning the number of desks for mobile workers.

To share, to pool, to touchdown: that is the question

The way in which the total number of workplaces used by a group is allocated can vary. The notion of a shared desk implies that two or perhaps more individuals have the use of a single desk. This is initially an appealing and simple way to manage the problem of space. Similar to the concept of a 'timeshare' holiday, this is a timeshare desk! The sharers can behave as if they owned the desk because their personal possessions can be stored at or near it, they can agree with the colleagues with whom they share when they have the right to use it, who fills up the empty stapler and whether to take each other's phone messages or tell callers when to phone again. The problem with this form of sharing is that some residual sense of ownership still operates. If each person's timetable cannot be fixed, then serious trouble can result. Coming into the office on an unplanned basis can produce the reaction 'Who's been sitting in MY chair?', or the more disruptive 'Get out of my chair.'

A pool of desks shared between a larger group of people, who may sit at any desk in the pool, can avoid this problem but only at the expense of insisting that no one has a desk of which they own even a part share. The pool needs to be the right size; it needs to be managed so that the bullies do not corner an 'own' desk where they always sit when they do come in; personal items have to be equally accessible to all the desks, yet not at any desk. Accessible smaller 'touchdown' desks can be provided for people who come in for very short periods. These are the equivalent of the high stool at the counter in the restaurant where a snack takes a few minutes, rather than the table suitable for a longer meal. Restaurateurs know that, to function properly, tables must be cleared and salt, pepper and sugar containers refilled. Some office organizations have taken similar steps for their liberated mobile workforce. Support staff replenish the stationery and supply the documents requested in advance by mobile workers. Not all managers are convinced that to provide and maintain communally owned staplers and other desk accessories is cost-effective. Perhaps the history of petty pilfering of office stationery items is too well remembered as an irritation and a betrayal of 'honest' behaviour, so that calculation is not made of how many staplers could be bought and stolen for the cost of a single desk or the cost of renting floor space on which to put it. The fact that it is no longer the stapler that staff would pilfer but the desktop computer has probably not been adequately considered either.

It is vitally important that personal storage for those who work at pooled desks is properly dealt with. Furniture manufacturers have only recenly started to consider the types of storage furniture suited to pooled desk arrangements. The mobile personal pedestal and the part share in a communal cupboard have not proved totally successful; new designs are emerging but are not yet widespread. Furniture available for this purpose is discussed in chapter 5.

Enclosed offices can be pooled as well. The provision of fewer offices than people who use them is far less widespread than desk sharing though it occurs. Andersen Consulting, the management consultancy arm of a large accountancy organization, has taken a radical step in this direction. In one of their USA locations there are enough consultants, previously entitled to an 'owned' office, to allow a pool, at a ratio of one office per five people, to function effectively. Each office is identical; each is well decorated, with attractive pictures, desk accessories and furniture. Just as consultants book hotel rooms in advance, so they book an office and, on arrival, find documents and mail already there and a telephone with their usual extension number on it. This system works only where there is a large number of cellular office users, most of whom are away a great deal. It also depends on effective secretarial back-up that enables the right files and papers to reach offices in advance.

Even more important than the details of furniture and accessories is the development of clear rules about how people should use the pool of desks or offices and systems to ensure that everyone can be contacted effectively as required. These demand a mixture of management and technical solutions. Communications systems, the telephone and message-transmission technologies, are being developed to serve situations where people need to be contacted in different locations, within or outside the office. These are part of the foundations of the virtual office.

The virtual office

> 'It doesn't matter whether you want to stay three months or just one day, whether you want the full office or just a token presence. Just walk in and you are in business.'
>
> Advertisement for Carlton, the Instant Office Network, 1991

The 'virtual office' relies on the idea that technology is now capable of routing communications effectively so that they can reach someone, no matter where they are, so seamlessly that the 'person at the other end' can behave as if he were contacting someone in an old-style office building. The old certainty of location is effectively replaced by the new certainty of reaching YOU, as your office is where you are. This is achieved at present by numerous strands of communications technology. Telephone systems can be rerouted to any location in a building if people stray from one desk or room to another, maintaining the extension number as an adjunct of a person, not of any particular telephone. Radio links can extend communication beyond the building to the mobile phone that the caller assumes is in the office. Electronic mail (e-mail) and voice mail allow slightly disjointed but effective two-way communication between people on the move. Network connections, rapid and high-volume transmission of data, the development of video links all enable people out of the office – or without an office – to seem as if they are in one. For a while a virtual office may be an apology for, or a concealment of, the fact of not being in a real one. In due course the term 'office' is likely to be replaced or to change its connotations. It will be neither possible *nor desirable* to pretend that wherever you are is 'virtually' an office. To be in an office akin to those of today will not be necessary for those companies that have shown by their experience that they do not need to be in such offices, that they function effectively in other modes. That some groups may remain in the type of office buildings currently familiar for a long time to come will not invalidate new working methods.

Many versions of virtual offices exist, known sometimes as 'executive suites'. Some of the earliest developed in big airports, where busy executives could pay for secretarial help, photocopy and fax documents and hire meeting space. They have spread to city centres and to suburbs, providing rooms, single or in suites, or sometimes only desks. Here an organization of twenty, or a one-man band, or the embryonic outpost of a large but distant parent company can access shared equipment and space for meetings, a shared reception and telephone-answering system and a complete smokescreen to hide the size of the organization or the identity of its next-door neighbour.

'We was robbed!'

If you can work out the essential infrastructure and operational rules for a particular business espousing new work practices and flexible approaches to office use, there is still a fundamental problem to be solved. That is the problem inherent in trying to change conventions and to create new relationships. Many people find it hard, even impossible, to feel positive about desk sharing/pooling or working in radically new ways with ground-breaking technology. The resistance is not simply to change. The difficulty is that the office is more than a job, the desk more than a tool for the task, and people feel deeply threatened by their loss. This is eloquently testified to by the people quoted below, six months after moving to a brand-new office with many improvements over the old one, who, as they are part of a group who have always spent three to four days per week out of the office, have had their desks pooled.

> *We was robbed! Why are we the only ones lumbered with this poor system? It wastes time, decreases feelings of personal involvement (I'm just a cog, I fit anywhere), reduces feelings of team involvement.*
>
> *I do not like the shared-desk system. I am adapting to it. I understand the reasons for it ... However, I think it is necessary for staff to have space that is their own. Work is an important part of most people's lives. It is their status, it is their source of livelihood, aspirations and fulfilment. It is a very insecure world subject to many changes. I think that having one's own little reasonably secure space that can be personalised to a degree is psychologically very important to most people. From that 'secure' space people can and do face 'the rest' with more confidence. Although I can't prove it, and I doubt anyone else can, I think that one of the reasons for so much sickness since we moved is because the 'secure' anchor has been removed. It is also a fact that many people use work as a 'safe' haven from the pressures of domestic life. Their space at work is theirs – not the family's. It helps to keep the 'stressors' in balance.*
>
> Questionnaire responses: staff in a newly refurbished office using desk pooling

Similarly people may be slow to take to voice messaging, find it hard to be unidentifiable by place. So the challenge is to find a way to realize the benefits of such a change and yet not throw the baby out with the bath water.

What is the office for, if everyone is working somewhere else?

In part it's what it was always for, a place to come to in which to work. As important as the possibility of working away from the office is the change in the way office work is actually carried out within offices. The advent of computers has meant that many office workers are far more productive but at the expense of being forced to adapt to using machines and subjected to discomfort and physical stress as a result. These, among other influences, have helped to create more awareness of what tasks people actually accomplish during their time in an office and how the tasks may differ in their physical requirements. People think, write, record and manipulate their own thoughts or information gleaned from other sources, talk on telephones or face to face, search files and do many other varied activities in the course of a working day. All of these things can, and do take place in offices. The variety has become more widespread, applicable to a larger proportion of the workforce. More productive people make higher demands on their bosses for interesting and varied work. Greater understanding of physical stress related to computer work has stimulated the belief that variety in tasks is important for health. Faster communications between people has fostered the growth of more complex work interactions and helped to emphasize the value of teamwork. These developments mean that it is no longer appropriate to assume that a single type of work-place, an office or desk in one place in the building, is the best provision for a member of staff in an office.

Staff in organizations that have advanced down the route of new technologies, new organizational patterns and new ways of working may operate in a variety of ways, at different times in the working day; for different tasks they may realistically need to move between distinct locations, suited to the activity of the moment. This sort of development changes the way offices are designed and equipped, and judged to be good places to work.

If it is accepted that the office building cannot be designed equally well for all functions, on what should it concentrate? The concept that attracts the media is that of the club, the place where people come together not only for planned meetings and face-to-face teamwork but also for the important serendipitous benefits of unexpected meetings and the exchange of apparently unrelated ideas. You are a member; you don't have to attend from nine to five. You are there from choice because it serves your needs. The business lounge, the business-class waiting room of an airport, has been used by some as the prototype of the office worker's club of the 1990s. The airline provides the receptionist who greets you, ensures that the formalities of travel are arranged and does not interrupt the relaxed pre-meeting meeting. Food and drink are available. Chairs are comfortable and informal, and they are near tables, allowing briefcases to be opened and their contents perused. Telephones can be used with your credit card if you do not happen to have your own mobile phone, and there are fax machines, newspapers to browse and, most important of all, other people like

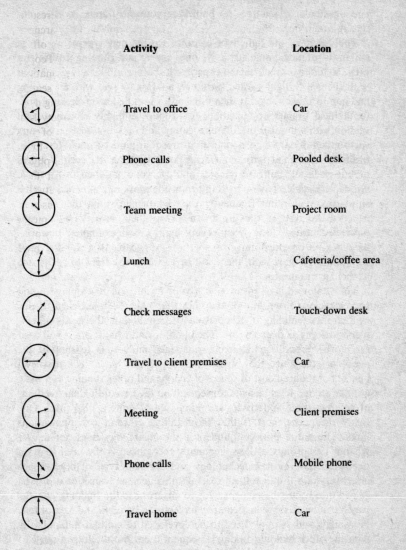

	Activity	Location
	Travel to office	Car
	Phone calls	Pooled desk
	Team meeting	Project room
	Lunch	Cafeteria/coffee area
	Check messages	Touch-down desk
	Travel to client premises	Car
	Meeting	Client premises
	Phone calls	Mobile phone
	Travel home	Car

Figure 1.4 Different work settings for different activities.

you on similar missions – no babies or young children. In all essentials it is an office.

The design of the right type of office for the new type of worker is still in its infancy. Some attractive ones are up and running. In Finland DEC initiated a much visited experimental office unlike any office seen until then, with light garden furniture, a swinging seat with an awning and comfortable nooks. It then went on to use the lessons learned and, for a local branch organization, to produce a highly effective small version with a number of different seating and desk options: easy chairs surrounded by tall green plants grouped around a small fountain, ordinary desks but with no storage or telephone, as each person's mobile pedestal stands to the side and everyone has their own mobile phone, and taller tables, to stand at while working, intended for the short-stay visitor but frequently used by people when they wish to observe the rest of the group and keep their own VDU screens discreetly turned away from prying eyes. Good examples, however, have not yet provided universal solutions applicable to a wide range of situations. To start with, there will be as many solutions to each issue as there are examples.

The vital need is to ensure that if your business is developing, or will soon develop, along any of the lines that have been sketched in this chapter, the building it occupies can accommodate the needs of new work patterns as they develop. The building and what it offers will need far more conscious and directed management if it is to support the needs of staff once they work in more flexible ways. The first-level benefits of reduced cost of space, of energy and other running expenses, and the second-level benefits consequent on the new individual freedoms of personal time and space, are purchased at quite a high price. One easily recognized cost is that of installing efficient communications links. The entire project founders if the technology does not deliver what it has promised. Less frequently recognized is the need to train people to use the new technology and the new type of office space effectively and to nurse them carefully through the transitional phases. A new need must be recognized – to ensure that the building and the way it can be used are immediately understood by users and memorable. New signs and symbols need to be developed to combat unfamiliarity with the office building among infrequent users and the loss of sense of personal or group identity. To meet this need requires knowledge and people: knowledge of how to provide and manage storage, how to choose the correct number and types of desks or offices, how to acknowledge rights and duties of staff in relation to these workplaces; people, such as receptionists, and back-up staff to help those who are rarely present but need to access the hub of communications in order to support their work. These back-up staff may get lonely, bored or confused by seeing some people only rarely, and their needs too must be considered.

IBM UK took a very broad and comprehensive look at new ways of working. They created the SMART (Space, Morale and Remote Technology) programme and worked as hard at the morale and remote technology elements as at the space issues. The early stages of the programme followed a strict set of project principles, important to the success of new ventures. Data-gathering in advance, to determine appropriate ratios of people to workplaces, was extensive. User needs were carefully investigated. Trials were implemented and feedback gathered. Then the SMART approach was ready to go live. The effects were monitored, and the roll-out continued, allowing new technology to be used more extensively and many unwanted buildings to be emptied and disposed of.

Their approach is one that needs to be considered for all such ground-breaking projects. Only when the ideas are common currency, when concepts such as pooling or ratios of desks to people are understood by managers and users alike, when the right furniture and telephone systems have been sold in their thousands, will it be easy to embark on changed ways of providing office space without careful data collection, user consultation and pilot trials.

Summary

This chapter helps to clarify how to accommodate your organization if it is in a position to exploit some of the new ways of working. It allows you to see whether you need a traditional office building or something very different. The effects of new technology on office work patterns is discussed in relation to their impact on buildings. This is of particular relevance to the types of organization listed at the start of the chapter.

Maximum publicity is being given to the concept of 'location-free' work. The development of communications technology first brought the office together and now is enabling it to drift apart. The extent to which this idea is accepted will vary according, in part, to how suitable it is for a particular organization.

'Telecommuting' describes the option to avoid the journey to the office by working elsewhere, be it at home or at a local office. Management does not always find it easy to accept that people will be sufficiently motivated to carry out their allotted tasks if they are not under its eye. Generally this has not been found to be a problem in practice. More of a difficulty is that isolation may not suit everyone, and not all homes provide a good work environment.

Observations show that in some organizations desks may be unoccupied as much as 80 per cent of the time. It is necessary to know what the actual (not the supposed) pattern of use is before making plans; this requires methods for systematic observation. The trends and prospects for future change are equally important. New ways of providing furniture and equipment are being sought. Ways to organize the office for those who use it only occasionally are still being developed. The temptation to arrange for two or more people to share a specific desk should be resisted. Where possible, a pool of desks, available to a larger number of people on a first-come-first-served basis, is more likely to work. Any innovative solution will require more management time to be devoted to it than the traditional one person-one desk. In an extreme situation some people may have a 'virtual' office a lot of the time and communications systems that enable them to simulate the fixed office when, in reality, they may be anywhere at all.

A new way of planning for people who are often out of the office may be well justified but is unlikely to be popular. It needs to be well prepared, implemented only for those to whom it is really suited and taken seriously by managers to the extent that they also use pooled space if at all possible. Even when accepted, the real sense of loss that people experience must be understood and taken into account. There must be real advantages for the individuals involved as well as for the organization. If undertaken merely as a space-saving exercise, 'hot desking' is not likely to be a success.

Whatever changes are undertaken, the specific solutions for technology, furniture, plan layout and management are crucial. These must be worked out carefully and based on good data.

2   Knowledge is Power

'It may be state of the art, but is it what we need?'

> *Influencing behaviour is almost all of what management is about, and buildings influence behaviour. Failure to wring every benefit out of the most expensive capital asset most companies ever have would not be countenanced in any other aspect of corporate life.*
>
> John A. Seiler, 'Architecture at Work', *Harvard Business Review*, Sept.–Oct. 1984, p. 120

Are you a prisoner in your own building, or does it serve you? How well do you know your building? The first requirement for making the most of an asset is to know what the asset is. The next is to know in what ways it may be used to your benefit. If you were asked a few basic questions about your building, could you answer them or, at least, get the right answer with a single telephone call? How big is it? How much space do you have? What does it cost you as a percentage of revenue and per person? When was it built, and with what form of construction? What kind of tenure do you have? Do you have an air-handling system and, if so, what type? Is your plant operating at optimum levels for your requirements? And so on. If information is not available, or is inaccurate, or is in the hands of others, you will have less power to make sensible decisions and be more likely to be manoeuvred down routes chosen by others, which may not suit your needs.

It is commonplace these days to read that a business's greatest asset is its staff – so much so that it seems impossible to believe that there was ever a time when managers did not know this. It is well understood that there is considerable investment in people, that they take time to train, both in the ways of the business and in specific knowledge and skills in their particular field. The armed forces, for example, know that it takes fifteen years to train a good officer. This being the case, one may justifiably wonder how they could ever have been so profligate as to throw away their investment by dismissing women officers when they became pregnant. The policy indicated that, at one time, the forces did not fully understand that their major asset is people. Such lack of understanding is no longer usual. Industry is increasingly knowledge-based, and it is people who have the monopoly on the use of knowledge, so their importance is accepted better than in the past.

After salaries, what costs most?

Buildings do. The capital cost of buildings is not ignored but is viewed as a necessary evil, as an outlay up-front or in the form of a loan or rent. Office buildings may also be treated as a potential crock of gold as a result of speculation in the property business. Neither view is complete; neither looks at the ways in which a building can best serve the needs of the organization. After staff salary costs, the next biggest bill for office-based organizations is that associated with buildings – renting, rating, running and repairing them. Accommodating each member of staff can cost between £1,500 and £10,000 per year. To make the best use of this inevitable expense takes some knowledge of buildings on the part of management. Companies change rapidly – this is becoming more and more of a truism – yet buildings last a long, long time. Buildings must continue, through many changes and adjustments, to be a valuable asset, to serve and protect organizations. They have the potential to do these things. Skill and understanding are needed to bring them about.

Yet business shelves in bookshops are strangely empty of texts that explain anything at all about buildings to managers of companies. Managers of the buildings themselves are somewhat better served, but they do not manage the business. The skills associated with management of people and understanding business cultures are naturally the most important, since people are a company's main asset and their biggest cost. None the less it seems reasonable that the next biggest cost item, the building, should not simply be regarded as a liability, a drain on resources. The scale of financial liability is considerable. An office may cost 10–20 per cent of company revenue annually to acquire, operate and repair. Its role as an asset is considerable. Its potential not only in the capital balance sheet but also as an influence on behaviour, as an enabler or inhibitor, as a tool to improve service to customers, as an influence on business cultures, should also be explored and understood in order to maximize benefits or, at least, reduce waste.

In the late 1980s, for a brief moment, the property market played a major role in financial planning and management in many businesses. This was a step beyond earlier booms because managers within indi-

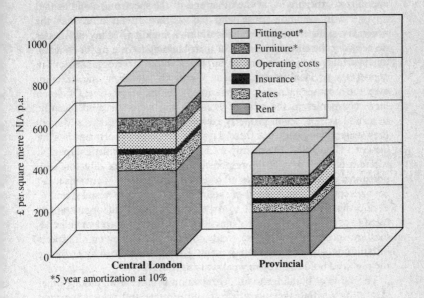

Figure 2.1   Fitting-out costs in the context of premises costs per annum.

Source: Bernard Williams Associates, *Facilities Economics*, Building Economics Bureau, Bromley, 1995, Fig. 6.2B.

vidual organizations, not merely property dealers and estate agents, became aware of the asset values represented by buildings as never before. Large profits were made from property deals. Some companies were bought simply to acquire, and then immediately sell, their under-valued property holdings. For a while it seemed as if the upward spiral of value could not be halted. Many drew dangerous conclusions from what they saw happening in the market-place. They acted as if their organizations could take on the role of a property-development business merely on the basis that they were building owners or occupiers.

All organizations employ staff with financial skills or have a group of advisers with whom they are in regular contact. Finance directors, usually some of the most senior people in an organization, are able to assess advice on leases, taxation issues and rents. However, here our concern is with the considerable gap in their knowledge of build-ings themselves and their contents. Generally these do not fall within the remit of senior management. Either senior management relies on specialized expertise or, at the other end of the spectrum, assumes that anyone with common sense who has worked in an office has the necessary skills to make decisions about a building. Many businesses do consider the efficient running of their building to be a major concern, and specialized expertise is often employed within large organizations in a property or facilities department. Generally, however, the status of even the most senior people in that area is comparatively low. Of eleven large companies to the west of London that were surveyed recently, none had its most senior property executive on the main board, although they generally agreed that these days the property department is a bit 'less of a Cinderella'. Frequently the role is shared in smaller companies, where it is often part of the responsibility of the finance director, with personnel or human resources involved to some extent. A current trend is to accept that management of the building is not core business and to decide that it should be left to experts in independent organizations hired to carry out the necessary functions. Facilities management companies are sprouting everywhere, ready to save you money on all aspects of building decisions and management. They probably can, but you are the one who holds the key to what you really need.

The value of buildings to an organization is influenced, among other things, by whether they are efficient, appropriate and project the right image to staff and clients. Senior managers need some knowledge of how such qualities may be achieved. They must be able to instruct and assess the specialists who understand buildings and interior fitting out and be able to check that decisions do not ignore important potential. Some of the vital characteristics of buildings can be readily measured, others less easily.

How big is it?

This sounds like a simple question – even simple-minded, so obvious that it must be unimportant. Not so. If it were so simple, everyone would have the right answer, but they do not. They often have no answer at all without asking their lawyer what they are paying rent for; and, if they do that, they may have no idea of what the answer really means. And it is not unimportant. Rent is usually related directly to area and is expressed in terms of pounds per square metre/square foot. Other costs, rates, daily running and maintenance, the cost-in-use are all dependent on the building size and design and can all be described in area-related terms. Value for money cannot be assessed in a vacuum; it concerns relative costs. Expression of cost per unit area allows relative costs for different buildings, and for different ways of running buildings, to be considered and the best ones for the purpose to be selected.

Information always helps people to make decisions. Consider energy costs. One of the easiest ways for an energy manager to achieve large savings for an organization is to learn how much energy is used (for example, to discover the peak electrical load that the company requires and to make sure that only the appropriate tariff is paid). Equally easily, money can be lost by, say, signing a long-term agreement for a rate based on inaccurate information, such as an assumed annual consumption that is higher than the actual one. The same is true of space. If total area is inaccurately measured, or if the two parties to a contract are not measuring the same things, someone (usually the occupier) gets a bad deal.

When considering space in buildings a plan drawing of the building is an important starting point. Drawings to a scale – any scale will do, provided it is stated on the drawings – that show the main building structure, the windows, the escape stairs, the lifts, the WCs, and, if possible, the electrical and other services are what is required. It does not matter if the partition and furniture layouts are not up to date. Changes in these are easily sketched on to a drawing that has the correct dimensions of the building's main features. Frequently managers have lost track of where suitable plans can be found in buildings a few years old, so that new ones have to be created from a fresh accurate survey. This is not difficult to do, but it costs time and money. It is astonishing how hard it often is to get hold of a proper scale drawing because, for example, 'The architect came from the Channel Islands and anyway went out of business, so we have no drawings of the building.' People who deal with leases are content with rudimentary drawings or none at all. Maintenance engineers often have simplified sketches of the building, with electrical or heating information superimposed diagrammatically, which are adequate for their needs but not useful for decisions about space.

Even with a good plan, measuring a building is not simple because it has many layers, like an onion. There is one size when you measure round the outside, another when you measure around the inside of the outside walls, another when you exclude the space taken up by 'cores', which contain essential ducts and plant rooms, lifts and fire stairs. The size of each layer of the onion is relevant for different reasons. Fortunately, there are rules that can be used to decide how each layer is defined. Some of the rules used in the UK emanate from the Royal Institute of Chartered Surveyors, where estate agents are born. Not surprisingly, these are the ones that matter most for rent. The inner layers are the ones that matter for the occupier, as they concern the areas that can be used for business purposes. Space planners and interior designers have been busy, in the last decade or so, refining rules that describe the inner layer.

Figure 2.2 indicates the different areas that are useful to measure on a building plan. The details of measurements of all the different layers need not be committed to memory, but the rules of thumb about efficiency, which express the relationship between the areas, are useful. Until you know the areas involved you cannot work out how space-efficient your building is.

It is instructive to check existing records of areas measured for different purposes and to ascertain that they have been clearly defined, that they match the areas described in the following paragraphs and that those that should be the same actually are. For example, is the amount of space measured for a cleaning contract the same as the area rented? If they are identical, were they both measured independently, or was one inaccurate measure copied from the other? If they differ, what is the reason? If the area cleaned is larger than that rented, are you cleaning someone else's space – say, the landlord's common areas? If so, is this reflected in rent or service charges? And so on. Someone must be sure that they know what areas have been measured before any of these questions make sense.

The first two items, core and structure, are givens in any building, once it has been designed. Their efficiency is of concern to the owner of the capital tied up in the building. The third, primary circulation, falls within the net lettable area (NLA)[1] – the rented area – and yet it cannot be used except to move around the building. The larger it is in relation to the lettable area, the more rent is effectively being paid for the usable area. The shape of a building, as well as how it is used, has an effect on the necessary primary circulation routes.

The next item, 'fit factor', is also influenced by the building design. 'Fit factor' is a term used here to indicate the space over and above the basic space allowance that is needed to 'fit' required uses into the building as a result of peculiarities of the building itself. It is not a standard term. 'Fit factor' is a nuisance, so the smaller it is the better. It is large where irregular shapes cannot accommodate sensible furniture

---

[1] Numerous versions of the terms used here may be found in other books and in the estate planning and management documents of any organization. The principles outlined here remain the same, though the terminology and precise area definitions can vary.

A building has many layers, like an onion:

Structure + core – walls, columns, plantrooms, stairs and lifts, WCs, lobbies
Primary circulation – main corridors, horizontal routes required for escape in case of fire
Fit factor – space that is unusable because of building peculiarities
Support space – for all the building: cafeteria, library, reprographics, conference suite
Ancillary space – for departments or groups: group files, local copier, project area
Work space – desks, offices and the local circulation to reach them

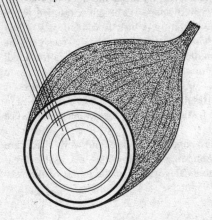

Main components of building area

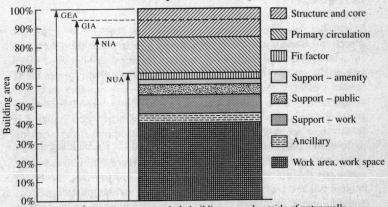

GROSS EXTERNAL AREA GEA whole building around outside of outer walls
GROSS INTERNAL AREA GIA whole building to inside of outer walls
NET INTERNAL AREA NIA gross internal area less all structure and cores
NET USABLE AREA NUA net internal area less primary circulation

Figure 2.2 Area measurements.

Source: Alexi Marmot Associates.

layouts, where perimeter space is wasted by intermittent radiators that prevent the use of a narrow fringe all round the space, where columns or structural walls break up useful areas into the wrong sizes. An example of the type of problem that occurs is seen in a typical 1980s building in London, with distinctive curved bay windows on all upper floors. When you get inside you find that the floor is raised by one step in the bays. The curved shape, although attractive, is in itself not much use for office furniture, which is fundamentally box shaped, so some space is inevitably wasted merely as a result of the shape of the floor. To make matters worse, the raised area is too small to use for a desk or small meeting table, so the whole bay is in effect wasted. Fit factor is often large in historic buildings. A delightful environment can result from room sizes, structure and many attractive architectural features that are inconvenient for office planning.

The last three area categories, support, ancillary and work space, are what the occupier wants the building for. How the 'net usable area' (NUA) is divided between these categories is in the hands of the user and will be considered in later chapters.

Is it efficient?

Space efficiency, thermal efficiency, maintainability and so on are all aspects of efficiency. Here space efficiency is at issue; the others are considered later. Space efficiency involves choosing well-designed space and making good use of it, *not* squeezing into space that is too small. It is always possible to cut down on area by providing minimal desks and no amenities. This is not efficient if it fails to deliver a good, productive working environment. Space efficiency is about how well a building is suited to office use, both for the occupants and for the working patterns of a particular organization.

The relationships of the areas identified in figure 2.2 are one way of measuring this efficiency. If the area on which you pay rent, the NLA, is large but the area you can actually use for accommodation of staff and equipment, the NUA, is very much smaller, then the building is inefficient for the user. The higher the rent paid per square metre, the worse is the value for money to the user of an inefficient building. As a rule of thumb, an acceptable building, from the tenants' point of view, is one in which the primary circulation represents between 15 and 20 per cent of the lettable area or, expressed another way, the ratio of usable to lettable is between 85 and 80 per cent.[2] Where the primary circulation is less than 15 per cent of the NLA the building is efficient. Where it is more than 20 per cent it is poor. The difference may seem small, but take 5 per cent of a 500-square-metre area of office space – that is, 25 square metres – at £200 per square metre per year (not an exceptionally high rent) and the saving on an 'efficient' over an 'inefficient' area is £5000, to be paid year after year. In addition, with an extra 25 square metres you could accommodate three or four more people. So space you cannot use is extremely expensive, in terms of both cash and opportunity lost. To justify the cumulative impact of paying for an inefficient building over many years, the building must offer other compensating factors, such as lower-than-average rent, terrific location, exceptional architectural quality, usable floors that are especially suited to departmental needs or a combination of many plus factors. The compensating factors need to be kept constantly under review to check that they are still valid – for example, that the rent stays below average, that the location is still excellent. The time to get the efficiency right is when making a move to a new or a refurbished building, as most of the relevant factors are fixed once the building is built. So if you got a bad bargain at your last move there may be little to be done about it. Working out the efficiency of an existing building is still worth while. Really understanding the process of collecting and using measurements is invaluable when it comes to a move, and doing it is the only way to understand it. Knowing just how good – or bad – your current building is may help you to make the decision about whether or not to move and will provide a benchmark against which to judge future options.

Other area-efficiency calculations can be made. The area of the whole building, the gross internal area (GIA), includes all the internal structure, walls and columns holding up the building inside the inner face of the outside walls, and the cores. If this area is very much larger than the area for which rent can be charged, then the building is inefficient for the owner. The larger the GIA, the more expensive (other things being equal) the building is to build and maintain. If it has a small lettable area, the capital outlay is not working as efficiently as that on one at the same rent level with a proportionately larger lettable area. For owner occupiers the gross is effectively the same as

[2] When primary circulation is 20 per cent of NUA it is only 15 per cent of NLA, so keep checking the figures if using the rules of thumb.

the lettable area, since that is what they are paying to run. But the two different measures of efficiency still need to be considered separately, based on the layers of the onion in figure 2.2.

Some rules of thumb are suggested below. These are for guidance rather than the last word on the subject:

owner efficiency	when the ratio of lettable to gross internal area is 80 per cent or more it is good, and when it is 70 per cent or less it is poor.
tenant efficiency	when the ratio of usable to lettable area is 85 per cent or more is good, and when it is 75 per cent or less it is poor
primary circulation	allow about 15 per cent additional space over and above the area required for work, ancillary and support activities. If you have a complicated floor plan, this percentage will increase. If you need much more than 20 per cent, a change of layout may be indicated
'fit factor'	3 per cent or less of lettable area is good; 5–10 per cent of lettable can easily happen. Over 10 per cent is worth worrying about
internal partitions	5 per cent of lettable area occupied by partitions might occur even in an open-plan building; 15 per cent of lettable area occupied by partitions could be the consequence of a highly cellularized building.

Does it do you credit?

The building does not need to be lavish for the answer to be 'yes'. Danger lurks for the organization whose chief executive responds to the suggestion that elegance, not opulence, should be the objective of a new building design by saying, 'There's nothing wrong with a bit of opulence if it is in the right place,' and then proceeds to specify a 40-square-metre office for himself with attached shower, WC and kitchenette, plus a boardroom rarely used and able to accommodate only a custom-designed, one-off, crescent-shaped boardroom table. (This particular organization ended up having to vacate its building within a couple of years. These special bits of tailor-made opulence proved the hardest part of the building to replan successfully for the leaner, fitter organization that took it over.) Office opulence may cost the director his job. The new London headquarters for the European Bank for

Reconstruction and Development were extravagantly designed and large sums were spent in changing what was the newly built, lavish reception area provided by the building owner. Once the cost was made public, the fired director no longer had the opportunity of enjoying his new office.

A building needs to be able to accommodate the evolving needs of a business, so that organizational change is not held back or distorted by its limitations. It needs to support people, not frustrate them. When a building cannot support the work that is being done there, because it is inadequate in size, shape, layout or management, it shows. Furniture tends to become disorganized, desks and shelves fill up with papers, the floor gets covered in piles of marginalized material. While it is not essential that the building be 'intelligent', it should signal to staff and visitors that they are valued and that their needs are well served. Its image should reinforce the impression that the organization wishes to make.

Image clearly resides in the reception area. That it is easy to find, sufficiently large, comfortable, has a good colour scheme, is clean and congenially lit and has enough chairs, access to WCs and perhaps coffee are characteristics that make a visitor feel good. They may have the same effect on staff, affording them pride in their organization and the expert attention it pays to the needs of its customers. Image cannot stop at the entrance and visitor areas. If the staff areas are, in stark contrast, dingy, cramped, positioned along murky passages, inadequately furnished, then the very features that make a visitor feel cherished will add to the frustration of the staff. They will feel that money has been spent in the wrong place. If a building looks very lavish, a small or a young or public-sector organization will not wish to occupy it. Their managers believe, probably correctly, that customers and auditors will think that money is being spent on the wrong things, the look of the place, rather than on high-quality staff. They seek a more ordinary but 'businesslike' look.

There are many factors that combine to make a building one that does you credit and makes staff and visitors feel that they are held in esteem: the amount of space given to each person, whether individuals have enclosed offices, whether the facilities available are suitable for the work people do, the type of amenities provided, the colours and finishes of the building and its furniture, the quality and amount of IT, the standard to which the building is cleaned and managed, whether it reflects people's wish to be responsible to the environment and a host of others. Many of these subjects are considered in subsequent chapters.

> '*Most people still consider the quality of accommodation a reflection of the esteem in which the firm holds them.*'
>
> '*There's no pride in these offices. It starts with the firm. It's shabby, so individuals accept clutter. It's a bloody shambles actually . . . You don't bring people into your office.*'
>
> Questionnaire responses – management consultant in large accountancy firm
>
> '*This is the first time since I've worked in this organisation that I've wanted to invite my wife and kids to see where I work.*'
>
> Comment made to a visiting senior manager during a review of new premises

Sound management decisions cannot be made solely on the basis of what people say they want, such as lots of space or everyone in their own office, but they must take account of how people feel. When organizations move or adapt their buildings, some, if not most, decisions are made to take account of change. These may seem to disadvantage many staff. Change is, in itself, often threatening rather than stimulating. To set about implementing change without knowing what people want is to start from a position of weakness, making it hard to carry out decisions in a way that convinces those that matter, and the staff in general, that they are indeed valued. Not to know what people are using the building for, not to understand how well they feel it supports their needs may be the start of making the wrong decision. Finding out how people feel about their place of work, and why, is an important part of managing it well. Ways to make sure that management knows include using questionnaires or suggestion boxes so that people can say what they think, holding workshops and group meetings, watching and collecting real information about what they do and where, asking staff to fill in diaries indicating where they are at different times of day, having people available who know how to listen, directly or in passing, and can act on what they hear. All these methods are used by various organizations to find out how people feel about and use the building and why. They are particularly valuable techniques to help plan for future needs and to create the brief for relocation (see chapter 9).

Does the building encourage communication?

The building plan can influence the ease with which people talk to each other. If you seek a highly interactive environment, steer away from buildings with features such as: long, dark corridors with enclosed offices on each side; fire doors that inhibit people in one wing of a building ever moving into another; a restaurant or cafeteria located inconveniently far from workspaces, or of unattractive design; stairs and lifts that are hard to find or badly designed so people will think twice before nipping down to another floor; security systems that demand digipads or card swipes on doors into every floor. Conversely, communication will be eased in buildings without many doors or with fire doors left open permanently (except in case of fire when their electromagnetic closures come into play); open plan stairs that invite people to travel between one floor and the next even for a very short conversation; buildings with an atrium where lots of activity occurs overlooked by people on other floors who can rush over to catch the person with whom they would like to chat; glass partitions separating enclosed offices from corridors so that you can readily see who is in and who is out; catering facilities that encourage people to eat in them; sufficient space in tea-making areas for an easy conversation to take place without being overheard. In short, seek buildings with few visual or mechanical barriers.

Is it a good shape for your organization?

The efficiencies intrinsic to the building as a whole, the various different areas available, are determined very largely by the design: the shape of each floor, the location of cores on those floors, the number of floors, the spacing and design of windows. These determine the 'fit factor' and primary circulation routes. Possible ways to use a building are also determined by size and shape. A long, thin bedroom might be suitable for bunks but would not set off a four-poster bed to advantage. Similarly, the shape of a building fixes some of the ways in which it can be planned. As an example, there is a building whose shape has very little going for it, on a West Country educational site, known as the Cheesebox. It is small, eight-sided, with a central column to support a frilly roof. It got its name because every room is shaped like a triangular wedge of processed cheese. There are very few possible ways of using it, as few activities are well suited to this dominant shape, and space is

Figure 2.3   Floor plates of a sample of offices in central London (drawn to a common scale).

likely to be wasted in most furniture arrangements. Strong shapes such as triangles, circles or hexagons for parts of or whole buildings share these problems, especially where dimensions are small.

Simple circulation routes waste less space. The routes must connect entrances to all activities and, vitally, in case of fire let people reach safe exits from wherever they are. The position of enclosed rooms affects possible routes, and sensible sizes and shapes for such rooms need to be considered when assessing the overall shape of the building. Even with its simple circulation the poor Cheesebox achieves only a poor efficiency level of 71 per cent. This is because it is so small. In a larger building of the same shape an identical route would be more efficient as well as serving larger, more useful and pleasant rooms.

There is an infinity of possible shapes despite the almost irresistible urge to think of office blocks as simple rectangles several storeys high.

The shape and size of a building can tell you a lot about how and when it was built and the underlying assumptions about the way it would be used. Buildings vary according to prevailing office technologies and the type of work layouts favoured, as well as the construction technologies available in the place and at the time of construction. The hallmark of office buildings erected since the 1980s is the atrium, an internal covered courtyard running vertically through the middle of the building. The atrium developed in response to the desire for construction economy – the walls around the atrium are cheap to build as they are not fully weatherproof or soundproof – and economy in air conditioning – the atrium is often not a fully conditioned environment. It is often designed as a grand and glamorous space and gives people working next to it a view – outside awareness in trade jargon. Where culture or the law demands that no one is ever farther from a window than the depth of one other person's workplace, or where natural ventilation is a prerequisite, a deep landscaped office is not a possibility. The building must be no more than, say, 12–15 metres from window to window. The financial dealing sector in London, New York, Frankfurt or Tokyo depends on the adrenalin rush that a large, busy group can create. Windows would be an undesirable distraction and very deep floor plates, perhaps 20–30 metres from window wall to window wall, are favoured. The maximum number of storeys that can be built depends on construction materials and methods, on lift technology and on the restrictions of planning departments and neighbours. The number of floors that may be desired by the building's owner depends on land values and that required by the occupiers on how well the organization can function when located on different floors. Buildings used for offices have often had previous uses. Stately homes, more modest urban houses, converted warehouses, old schools are all used, with and without extensions. Many of the construction and planning details are very different from those of buildings purpose-designed as offices. They may have unusual room sizes, types of window, floor-to-ceiling heights and, of course, services. Sometimes they are of historic interest, with restrictions on how many alterations are permissible, but people show great ingenuity in converting them to offices.

Understanding whether the shape of a building is suitable for an organization's needs is a prerequisite to choosing the right one or finding the right way to use an existing one. A major retailer leased office space in a well-located building with a hidden disadvantage: the shape of the site. This led to an irregular, seven-sided courtyard building. It was laid out with many small individual offices, leaving inefficient areas for open-plan use. A reassessment of the spatial properties of the building revolutionized the floor layouts. After replanning and changing the circulation to improve the space efficiency, the response of the users was extremely positive – more people were accommodated, with more light, in more attractive space.

One young and rapidly growing company took on a five-storey building. Each floor was big enough for a single department, and the ground floor was suitable for shared facilities and reception. Occupying this building 'killed the company by slow death', according to a manager who left while it was dying, as separation by floor prevented the vital interaction needed so much during the period of change and growth. The building it needed would have allowed several, if not all, departments to be together on one floor, with additional space for future growth. Some sacrifices would almost certainly have been required to achieve this – for example, the company might have elected to accept loss of identity or prestige by accepting 'a tenancy in a larger building rather than ownership of a whole one or a less central location in order to be able to afford enough space for growth and change. The priorities were wrong when the choice was made because the decision-makers were unaware of the effect that an inappropriate building can have.

The decision to create a particular shape for a new building is complex and influenced by many considerations. It is essential to review a given shape and evaluate the consequences that it has for an organization, certainly before embarking on a major building project but even for a building that you are not planning to change immediately, as evaluation may indicate things that could be improved later, when an opportunity arises. There are a number of basic spatial properties to consider. The more important ones are covered here, though this is indicative rather than an exhaustive list.

● *Location and size of cores, entrances and fire stairs*
  Can the entrances serve separate organizations and make each feel they have a real identity? Do the positions of fire stairs relate well to the natural locations of primary circulation routes? Do the cores break up the space so that you never get the benefit of the maximum

dimensions and areas? Are the cores adequate in size and planning to contain all the services, such as ducts, cupboards, and WCs that are needed to sustain the building?

● *Depth of the floor plate – distance from window to window or to blind wall*

How many people can work near windows with the type of layout you need? If the space is deep – over, say, 18 metres between window walls – so that many people are far from windows, are there adequate compensations, such as being able to accommodate large groups or easy communication between groups? Can the inner areas be reached by the building services? Will ventilation be adequate? Can enough cables reach the positions where they will be needed?

● *Spacing of structure*

Is there always a column in the way of the desk arrangement you want to create or a window that cannot be subdivided when partitions need to be relocated? Is the clear space between fixed bits of structure suitable for groups of desks? Does the geometry of the plan or the windows mean that rooms can only be an awkward shape, too small to be useful or so large that they are wasteful? Generally a grid that breaks down to 1.5-metre lengths, both in plan and on the window elevation, is fairly flexible; 1.2 metres can make planning difficult; and a larger one, such as 2.0 metres, can lead to over-lavish rooms when partitions are planned.

● *Structure and fabric*

Is the construction sound? Does it incorporate potential problems, such as the difficulty of introducing cable routes, the presence of asbestos or other characteristics needing remedial attention? Will it withstand bomb attacks? Are windows double-glazed? Are the external fabric, walls, roof and windows in good repair?

● *Circulation routes*

Can simple routes be planned without kinks and dog-legs? Can main routes be left open with fire doors held on magnetic closures? Are there wasteful parallel circulation routes in spaces requiring only one? What percentage of the overall area on a typical floor will have to be occupied by the primary circulation route? Is the building efficient? Can appropriate security access points be incorporated?

● *Edges, corners and dead ends – 'fit factor'*

A large 'fit factor' (a lot of space you cannot use because of details in the way the building is designed) is undesirable. An allowance needs to be made for some unusable space, but if too many factors combine, the penalties may be too great. A small test layout of half a dozen desks or rooms the way you want them can help to show up unsuspected problems of fit. Do power and telephone cables routes make the fit bad by preventing desks being placed wherever they may be needed?

● *Subdivision*
Can room sizes vary, and are they suited to the organization's needs? Check what the largest area of contiguous space will be and the smallest. Small increments in the length or depth of a space, resulting overall in a larger area, may not be particularly helpful in accommodating more people, as furniture comes only in a limited range of sizes. To fit in one more person the extra dimensions have to be as big as a desk plus chair and its access. At the detailed level, can suitable room sizes be created, and can they be located in such a way that people in open-plan areas are not deprived of direct natural light?

Can it adapt? Is it the right shape for the future

These issues are as important as any absolute measures of size or efficiency. Management literature stresses the great changes likely to be experienced by the types of business that are survivors. Some of the changes will result in their seeking different ways to use office buildings, even when there are no significant changes in staff numbers. The characteristics of shape need to be considered in terms not only of the use initially intended but also of whether they allow alternative scenarios with reasonable ease. Many of the different issues that become important as organizations change – such as alterations in space standards, the amount and type of cellularization, whether 'hot desking' will suit some or all of the staff, the introduction of new IT systems or additional amenity areas – are considered in detail in other chapters. The ease with which any of these can be inserted into a building, and can continue to be fine-tuned to the organizational needs of the moment, relates to the design, the shape overall and in its parts and the details of grids and service routes.

If your building turns out to be inefficient, inappropriate, unadaptable or giving you a bad name, should you fix it or move? If you decide to move, chapter 9 is about relocation, but the chapters that follow this one explore in more detail various aspects of buildings that will help you to understand what decisions are needed to achieve maximum benefits from your building, whether you stay put or relocate.

Summary

This chapter gives you technical guidance to help you to decide if your buildings are efficient and suitable for your organization. As a good manager you need to know something about buildings. Buildings represent a cost of 10–20 per cent of revenue for a business. You need to understand how to make good use of them. Having the right information available when you need it is a key part of good management and decision-making.

How much space you use, and what it costs, is basic information. Whether your building is space-efficient, spatially appropriate and projects the right image is important additional ammunition. A plan of the building is a fundamental tool for the purpose of good space information. Size is measured by specific rules that must be applied consistently if comparisons and targets are to be useful. Efficiency ratios are helpful as targets. As an owner you need to seek a ratio of 85 per cent of lettable to gross area. As a user you need a ratio of 80 per cent or more of usable to lettable area.

To be exploited as a positive asset a building must make staff and visitors feel good rather than frustrated or undervalued. There are many management tools and techniques for discovering how to achieve this. The answers may sometimes be unexpected. The skill lies in matching the desired to the possible.

The size and number of floors need to be suitable for the groups and activities that they accommodate. There is more to a suitable building than getting that bit right. Convenient entrances and routes in the building, access to windows, possible ways to carve up and subdivide space, the likelihood of wasting floor area – all relate to detailed aspects of the shape as well as to the general topology of the building. Without trying to know all the answers, a good manager must know the type of questions to ask about the different aspects of shape: cores, depth, structural grid, 'fit factor', circulation, subdivision. These issues are particularly important when changes are made. Different ways of using the available space, the potential adaptability of the building, must also be considered.

3 Levelling the Space Pyramid

DARIUS, after Messrs Carroll and Tenniel.

Alice somehow sensed that her company's space standards were inappropriate

The space pyramid

Remember the last time you caught an aeroplane and sat in economy class – knees jammed up against the back of the seat in front, opening the newspaper on to the lap of your neighbour, wondering where to put your second foot after storing your bag under the seat in front? Didn't you feel wonderful that time you flew first class? Obviously there was more service, more hostess time, better cuisine, leg rests, your own video and telephone. You were not just more comfortable, you had *more than the others*.

One of the big questions every organization must answer is: how much space does each person merit? The cost of space per person is overtly reflected in different situations. Airline seats in the super-Apex economy section of the holiday charter night flight are much cheaper than those of Concorde's first class. Part of the reason for that, you may say, is because of speed and convenience of service. But first-class seats on any train or plane are also more generous than standard or basic ones. Here the cost does not reflect a difference in speed and convenience. Space, as well as speed, has a price set on it by the transport business.

In hospital wards the average area given to a patient varies. The bed itself occupies about 2 square metres. It is the space around it that varies. A Nightingale hospital ward, with rows of beds in open plan, is often used for routine cases. The needs of a patient are met in a basic way. In this setting the average space occupied by the bed and its surrounding space, including circulation, is about 9 square metres. In intensive care, where far more equipment is needed around a bed and where more staff are present, the area per patient increases to about twice that in the Nightingale ward – up to 18 square metres. Different space standards reflect the needs of the job. A private room, for medical reasons, is only provided for patients whose condition needs supervision or isolation. A private room can well take up three times the basic space if it also includes a private bathroom. It is provided for people who are willing to pay for privacy because they want it. Similar distinctions can be seen in hotels. A basic hotel room is not much larger than the bed and the dressing table. One that is not blessed with an *en suite* bathroom is cheaper than one that is. The bridal suite, as its name implies, is a whole suite of rooms, at a price.

Should offices be planned so that the amount of space given to each individual reflects their worth to the organization? And, if this is so, how is worth measured? Does seniority automatically confer higher worth? Do status and authority need the support of extra space? Should higher responsibility be rewarded by an acknowledged privilege – extra space? Manifestly different amounts of space are allocated to different people in an office, so extra money is being paid to support those with the larger areas. In a large UK office-based organization in the late 1980s there was a sixfold differential in both salary and space allocation between the lowest and the highest grades, suggesting that space and salary were comparable measures of worth. The space in this organization was carefully assessed on a cost-per-square-metre basis, so the most highly paid people were clearly making personal use of a much larger share of the accommodation cost. That same organization started to rationalize space standards in the 1990s, so that relative space costs no longer matched salary. How far have the implications of the cost of space per person begun to have an influence on what organizations demand from their office buildings? How far should they? What are the space standards in your own organization, and have they responded to pressures of planning efficiency and cost per person?

Space standards

A standard is 'an accepted example of something against which others are judged or measured'.[1] A space standard defines how much space, how much of the area in the building, is given to each person working there. Standards have value as guides to estimating the size of building that an organization should have, as design aids for a new project, as management tools to control the waste of space and as ways to safeguard the interests of individuals.

The discipline of space planning, in which designers concentrate on planning the interiors of buildings – often, though by no means always, office buildings – has developed in importance and has refined its

[1] *Collins English Dictionary.*

working methods. This means that the concept of space standards has become increasingly important and useful to designers in the two tasks of assessing overall space requirements for organizations and planning the use of buildings at a detailed level. Designers use space standards as a convenient aid for decision-making in both these tasks. They are delighted to turn to a document provided by the user organization that lays down the rules about who gets what. Such documents are not likely to exist in small organizations, though they are fairly common in large, mature ones. The politics of who gets how much space, decisions about how much is the right amount, and why, need to be codified to create such documents. This process provides an opportunity to assess whether the right priorities are being met.

Deciding on the organization's space standards is one way of making sure that an office building is used to its best advantage, as it reduces the likelihood of wasteful, unproductive, *ad hoc* decisions about space. Standards should, however, be seen as guidance, not as rights cast in concrete, even though one of their uses is to safeguard individuals from overcrowding and inadequate provision. In some situations they cannot be met exactly, and then there is the possibility that they will be used as a lever by those who wish to find fault. This is not a reason for doing without them, but it is an incentive to devise a sensible set of standards allied to an agreed approach to flexibility in their use.

Average lettable area per person

The simplest standard to guide an organization on how much space it requires is the average NLA that is required per person. This figure bears little resemblance to the area in which each person has to work, the workplace or the office, which is considered later in this chapter. As seen in figure 2.2, the lettable area includes support and ancillary space – which are discussed later in this chapter and in chapter 7 – as well as primary circulation (see chapter 1) and all the working areas. The average is reached by dividing the whole lettable area by the number of people working in the building. Average lettable area per person varies considerably. When working areas are planned with identical desk and office layouts, an organization with high requirements for support or ancillary areas uses more space per person than one that provides less space for these. Individual working areas also affect the overall average, as they vary between organizations; proportions of large and small are different, and in some not everyone has a desk of his or her own (see chapter 1).

The range of average space per person found in different offices is wide. This is true even within a particular type of organization, such as investment banks or solicitors' offices. The lower end of the scale is represented by about 9–10 square metres lettable area per person, implying modest working areas for each, few senior people in the office, few amenities and perhaps a degree of desk sharing. At the high end is an average area of around 35 square metres per person, nearly four times as much, implying large amounts of space for each individual and lavish shared space and amenities. These differences arise from different company styles, organizational needs and building decisions as well as from different national practices. The smaller allowance is not intrinsically better or worse, though it is by definition cheaper. It may or may not be appropriate for a specific organization. In the UK an average lettable area per person of about 15 square metres is fairly typical for a medium-sized organization with a range of different levels of seniority in the staff. In Scandinavian countries 30 square metres is not atypical.

If the average space per person is excessive, it can incur considerable extra costs. For a hundred people, each reduction in the average lettable area per person of 1 square metre saves not only the initial capital or rental outlay on 100 square metres but also running costs each year and periodic upgrade costs. This mounts up fast to a worthwhile saving when construction costs are £600 per square metre and running costs are, say, £50 per square metre per year. An efficient building delivers a lower average area per person. Space can be sensibly reduced without squeezing individual areas or being stingy with necessary support areas or desirable amenities, by systematically reducing *ad hoc* decisions and by planning the relationships of the individual work areas carefully, avoiding typical space wasters such as, for example, double circulation routes.

Space standards: many, a few or one standard for all?

The other use of the term 'space standards' indicates the area allowance for each person in any part of the office building. This is the area taken up by the 'footprint' of the working furniture, the desk, chair, storage and the access route to get to and use them. It is shown by a plan view of the space taken up by the items of furniture or the size of the personal enclosed office. It is associated with the net usable area rather than the lettable area. Primary circulation is not included in the workplace 'footprint'. For most organizations the way in which a job has been defined is linked indissolubly to grade or status. Generally the higher the grade, the larger the amount of space people are given, the larger their space standard – the 'footprint' of their workplace or room size. Space is often taken to be an entitlement, particularly where there are active unions and the more so if the space is called a standard. If you are a customer service manager, should you expect a larger amount of space than a customer service assistant? Should it be different if you have many or only one person working for you? What should any difference in space allowance be based on for these two or any other people? Is a standard an entitlement for staff, a goal for the organization to aspire to or a convenient way to calculate general ideas that need bear no direct relationship to the specific area occupied by particular individuals once layouts are planned?

Three different approaches can be adopted when deciding individual space standards. The outcome of the different approaches is shown in figure 3.1. Hierarchy may be of great significance to all aspects of the organization, so it is expressed in space standards as well as job titles, grade numbers and, perhaps, location within the building, degree of enclosure, access to amenities, number of days' annual leave and so on. With a long list of different grades there may be many individual standards – ten or more. Another approach is to reduce the number to a few, differentiated perhaps on the basis of the specific job requirements of individuals, which results in between three and five different standards. This approach implies not that there is no hierarchy but that seniority or responsibility are not recognized through allocation of space. Another approach allows all individuals identical space to work in, a single space standard. This is how, for example, a typical headquarters building in Stockholm might be planned, giving each person a small individual office of about 11 square metres. One young UK company active in the telecommunications business gives all but the seven top people an equal open plan workstation of around 6 square metres.

When grade sets the standards

Once upon a time, O best beloved (not so long ago), grade was a widely, almost universally, accepted way to establish space standards. Until recently all the space occupied by central-government departments throughout the UK was managed by a single department, the Property Services Agency, using a single set of rules applied to 600,000 people.

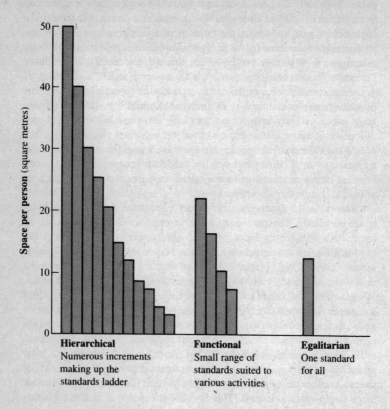

Figure 3.1   Three ranges of space standards.
Source: Alexi Marmot Associates.

At that time the British Civil Service provided an excellent and well-documented example of grade setting the standard. There was an entire 'suite' of space standards to match the full range of administrative and executive grades. There were eleven main standards and a total of twenty-two, including those for specialist jobs. They were expressed as ranges, recognizing that a precise area cannot always be easily granted because of differences in buildings. In the main they did not overlap. The largest size to which one grade was entitled was usually less than, or at best equal to, the smallest size available to the person on the next rung up the ladder. A clear distinction in space allowance was made between grades. The top standard was about 50 square metres, the lowest around 4 square metres. The actual sizes were decided in the days before metrication, and at the time the increments must have looked tidy. They were in the order of 50–100 square feet at a time. A casual glance at the list could deceive you into believing it was logical. Translated into metres, it looks a little more arbitrary. Ranges like 8.3–9.7 square metres are not memorable, are hard to manipulate and do not intuitively seem likely to fit into buildings designed with regular grids and bays. So did they represent a truth about the precise relation of space to grade that needed to be retained?

A distinction based on grade does have its uses. Promotion can be marked by an upgrade in standards, so fellow members of the office area are subtly made aware of enhanced status. Space can be thought of as a perk, so the pay rise may possibly be smaller. However, some of the attendant disadvantages can be ignored only if buildings are treated as 'free goods'. When someone is promoted, under an agreed set of space standards the higher grade rates a larger space. To provide this can be disruptive, especially if walls have to be moved. The disruption caused by a single promotion, however, is often insignificant. As promotion may mean a change of department, it is likely that a space of the right size has just been vacated, causing the need for the promotion and eliminating the need to change desk layouts or partitions. Larger-scale changes, related to general reorganization, major growth (or decline) or market shifts, are more complicated. As groups evolve, the mix of grades does not remain static, so either people have to use standards that are, in fact, not the ones applicable to their grades, thus nullifying the point of the standards, or changes have to be made overall to take account of the grade changes, which cost time and money. Many organizations that have experienced dramatic change, or anticipate upheaval in the future, have re-examined their approach to the number of standards they are using, reducing the number from, say, eight to around four or fewer.

'Less is more'

Less – in other words, fewer rather than smaller – standards make the office **more** flexible and **more** cost effective.

Reorganization of the office layout, so that standards are adhered to in the event of organizational changes, does not necessarily happen at each change, but where it does happen it is costly and is not necessarily justified. 'Churn' is the name given to the relocation of people within a building. Annual churn of 100 per cent is a way of saying that, on average, each person moves to a new desk in the same building, or to another building, once a year. The rate can be higher than 100 per cent, implying that some people move twice or more in the year. High churn rates are common in rapidly changing organizations, and some reorganization of the layout is bound to be needed in these cases. In 1993, in IBM's UK headquarters building the churn rate was about 66 per cent, that is, about 2,000 people moved out of 3,000, an average of about forty people every week throughout the year. A major finance and insurance company in the 'golden triangle' west of London nearly fell apart in a year when its churn rate was 190 per cent and most of its 3,000 staff moved twice in one year.

Office moves are expensive. They involve moving desks, reorganizing telephones and computers, sorting our relocated storage units and moving files. This can cost in the order of £2,000 per person moved. Part of this cost is incurred because disruptive moves should be, and usually are, done at the weekend, which entails payment at double and triple time for communications specialists as well as removal men. Fortunately these days moves can cost much less. If workplaces are generally the same size, moves become both cheaper and less disruptive and can even be carried out during the working day. Moving people around simply involves a small hiatus while the telephone numbers are rerouted at a switchboard, so that Jones keeps his extension number when he moves, taking a short time to wheel a pedestal full of files to his new location. In this situation the cost falls to an acceptable £100 per head or lower, depending on the building and the types of service that have to be rerouted. Uniformity of servicing to desks can be an additional cost-saver where the capital outlay can be justified. Even with reasonable costs per person, the disruption of churn needs to be controlled.

A reduced range of standards allows flexibility that is more than merely physical. When there are fewer formal distinctions it is less significant if individuals deviate a little from the standard. If the same standard applies to many grades, then slight variations do not carry overtones of promotion or demotion. Reshaping work groups need not have so many barriers to acceptance. It can happen when business requirements dictate. It does not have to wait while large sums are saved to pay for it, or while prolonged negotiations take place with staff who may resist a different space allowance for themselves or rail against the fact that their neighbours are going to get more space than in the last layout.

However, fewer standards are more significant. Where there are few well-differentiated standards, the differences are clear for all to see, and, if wrongly applied, the effects are obvious. If they are inappropriate, everyone is affected. If standards are too small, overall performance in the office may be badly affected; opportunities to accommodate minor changes in staff numbers by slipping in an extra desk or two may be inhibited; and morale may be low. If they are too large, the additional amount of space consumed by the organization rapidly adds up to a big rent and running-cost bill.

A shallower pyramid

The organizations that will survive and prosper are described in management literature as likely to be leaner and meaner. For many this implies a reduction in the layers of hierarchy they have inherited. Being meaner, they also appreciate the cost benefits of a reduced number of space standards in relation to office planning. So in many of these organizations the hierarchy is becoming flatter and the space pyramid shallower. The trend is towards fewer spaces standards, with a smaller differential between the lowest and the highest. Even where the hierarchy remains, several levels are given the same space standards. The British Civil Service, for example, has reviewed its many-layered space standards. Individual ministries, when questioned in 1990, indicated that they either had made, or would soon be making, changes in their standards, particularly by reducing the number of standards, although grade differences would remain unaffected. They will follow the lead of many of the larger commercial organizations. Reduced disruption and cost have helped to establish the logic of having fewer standards, less upheaval as group structures and numbers change, less wasted space where the standards were larger than necessary in order to signal status differential. Typically, a forward-looking commercial organization has three to five different space standards, matching a shallower hierarchical pyramid, as indicated in figure 3.2.

Changing space standards can seem, these days, to be synonymous with reducing them. A reduction in the number of standards, creating a shallower pyramid, is used as an opportunity to seek a lower common denominator. There is a danger in this. Standards should reflect the work to be done at the relevant workplace and should not fall below reasonable levels any more than they can be justified at exceptionally high levels. A natural swing of the pendulum, as well as a striving for cost efficiency, is a possible reason why changes in space standards tend

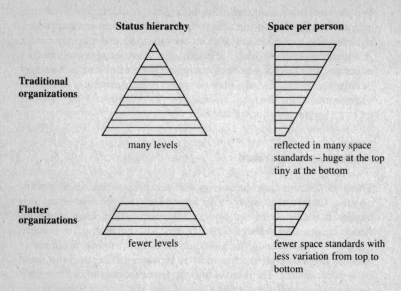

Status hierarchy   **Space per person**

Traditional organizations

many levels

reflected in many space standards – huge at the top tiny at the bottom

Flatter organizations

fewer levels

fewer space standards with less variation from top to bottom

Figure 3.2   Status and space pyramids.
Source: Alexi Marmot Associates.

to reduce work areas. The last few decades have witnessed an increase in average space per person. Figures collected for offices in the City of London, for example, show a 40 per cent increase in space per person over a twenty-year period, so perhaps it is time to tighten belts a little. This increase reflects larger individual workplace standards, designed to accommodate computers at individual desks, but increased ancillary and support space have been more important overall.

Typical workplace standards

Buildings are now expected to perform more efficiently on behalf of the occupiers. Setting space standards sensibly, and then sticking to them, is a way of ensuring this. What is included in a space standard? How do you know when a standard is sensible?

A hierarchical approach to space standards is still common in very traditional UK organizations. It makes a clear statement to staff and visitors about relative status and perceived worth, and in a modern context it gives a poor impression.

A local council department occupied an old building with gracious rooms. On each of two floors there was a room of identical size and shape with a bay window. The one on the upper level had a view of a historic town centre, and was occupied by the head of department. In the room below, differing only by having a less dramatic view, sixteen members of the department were crowded.

The smallest amount of space a person can occupy in an office, pursuing the analogy with the 2-square-metre hospital bed, is about half a square metre, which is taken up by a person sitting on a chair. To this must be added the space around the person. Just as in a hospital, it may vary. Regulations prevent exploitation and overcrowding. In the UK, 1993 guidance from the Health and Safety Executive asks for a minimum volume per person of 11 cubic metres, which in typical offices would imply an average floor area of about 4.6 square metres. This is based not on a concept of the space needed for the job but on consideration of hazards to life; it is to ensure adequate ventilation, to provide room to escape in case of fire, to create a space that is not too stressful.

Any sensible organization provides adequate space for doing the job. The space needed at a workplace for most jobs in offices must accommodate a desk, a chair and maybe some storage, as well as allowing the occupant an access route to their particular desk once they leave the main office circulation routes. In addition to paper- or computer-based tasks carried out individually, space is often expected to accommodate shared activities for which several people need to meet together to discuss ideas or to use the paper- and equipment-based information held at the desk. The space required by a simple workstation, for a single task done by a person who does not spend all his working day in that location, is surprisingly small. A bank teller's workstation at the cash counter is used for short spells of time and can be as small as 1 or 2 square metres. A workspace used for most of the day needs to be larger – say, between 4 and 6 square metres. A desk for a manager who has to hold small, informal meetings around the desk needs even more space. The fashionable 'tear-drop'-style desk additions, which are designed for these sort of meetings, create a 'footprint' that takes up about 9 square metres. Where a person needs enclosure it can rarely be provided sensibly in that small space, though this might be enough for a researcher's cubicle in a university. In an office setting someone needing enclosure generally requires more space to accommodate special requirements like working on extensive confidential paperwork or holding frequent meetings for more than three people. These activities can take place comfortably in about 12 or 15 square metres. When still more space is 'needed' for a single person it falls into the category of status-related space. Sometimes this is appropriate for particular situations – for example, to create a necessary atmosphere of control, confidence and confidentiality. Often it is not.

The footprints illustrated in figure 3.3 have the advantage of being modular; that is, they fit together easily and can be exchanged when numbers change. Two 6-square-metre workplaces can be created when a 12-square-metre office is eliminated or vice versa. Three of the smaller size are equivalent in area to two at 9 square metres. Modularity is not essential, and different areas may be chosen as standards for many reasons. However, where it can be achieved, especially if the areas can easily be created within the building grids, the interchangeability of spaces can be a significant help for replanning.

Ancillary and support areas

As well as the 'footprints' of individual workplaces there are areas shared by groups, called here 'ancillary' areas. When a service, such as a library or a computer suite or a reprographics facility, is there for the benefit of all the organization, it is called 'support' (see figure 2.2). Ancillary areas that are generally needed near working groups include storage accessed by all group members, coat cupboards, equipment such as photocopiers, shared computers, faxes and fiche readers, which are used by all but belong to no particular individual. Each group has different requirements; the areas needed must be assessed for each organization and each type of group. Typically, ancillary areas add between 0.5 and 1 square metre per person to the space requirement in the working areas. In one organization the staff dubbed the local support zone for everyone in one area of the building the 'village pump'. It contains items such as copiers, faxes and shared printers as well as vending machines and notice boards. It is acknowledged as a necessary fount of information and local gossip. Modularity is useful for ancillary or support areas as well. If they can share dimensions with the workplace standards, this further increases flexibility. If a 12-square-metre area can contain equally well an enclosed office, a photocopier and a stationery area, the 'village pump', a computer store room or a library facility, then as one requirement increases and another shrinks the spaces can be interchanged. The areas taken up by work-

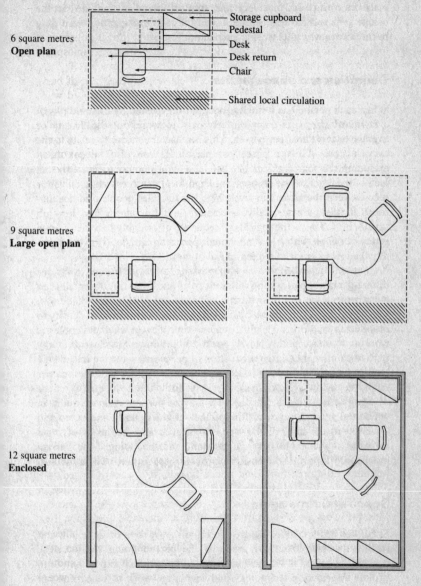

Figure 3.3 Typical workplace footprints.
Source: Alexi Marmot Associates.

place footprints and ancillary and support space are included in the usable area and have to be established for each organization according to the way in which its work is carried out.

Densities and space audits

When each person has a single space that they generally use, and it is of a standard size, it is comparatively easy to work out the density or average lettable area per person. This is a useful concept to relate to the average cost of office space per person. It can also be calculated excluding the shared things like cafeterias and photocopiers to give an idea of local density of occupation. High local densities, while they may help to keep the adrenalin levels high for telesales people and dealing-room junkies, are generally associated with low status and low job satisfaction. This is the logical consequence of bringing together a large group of people with a low individual space standard, who are tradition-ally the lowest grade in a hierarchical organization.

Chapter 1 described new ways of working for people housed in various different places, performing different roles and even not doing all their work in the office. For them the concept of density is no longer what it was. Global averages can still be calculated, but the relationship of density to office costs, or workers' health, or a real-time view of whether people are working in unacceptably closely packed situations is less clear. If at any particular moment a large proportion of people are working outside the building in which they are based, then a small average lettable area per employee, a low average space cost, says little about the quality of the working area. A more detailed view may be needed. A space audit, in which the space being used for specific activities can be measured and reviewed in the light of the type, importance and frequency of those activities, is a valuable tool for understanding the building. Time is now a much more important dimension in providing space than it was in the past.

Space and time again

Space has become more closely related to the work to be done in it and further divorced from the grade of the person doing the job. The concepts involved in the new ways of working, which expect people to exploit information technology and encourage work to be carried out when and where it is most suitable, have been combined with ideas about simplification that permit flexibility and cost control. From this has developed the concept of spaces for particular tasks: areas or rooms that have no particular individual's name attached to them, typical amounts of space for typical activities, not individual allowances for each member of the clerical, managerial or professional staff. Common terms in space planning today are 'quiet rooms', 'war rooms', 'project rooms', 'team areas', 'group bases', 'work lounges'. All these apply to spaces used by people for different tasks at different times and in different combinations.

It is suddenly more complicated. This approach allows office buildings to be viewed in the same way as, say, hospitals or universities. In these sorts of organization spaces are assigned to different activities that are not always participated in by the same people. Conversely, people are liable to use different spaces at different times. Offices have begun to behave more like these sorts of organization. It is now necessary to consider how much time people spend in a traditional workplace, what part of their function is carried out there and how large the area should be to fulfil this function. Standards for all the other spaces required by the organization must be considered. To provide enough, but not too much, space for any activity requires a secure knowledge of use patterns, so that a mismatch between need and available space happens only on an acceptable number of occasions and in circumstances in which an alternative solution can be provided. If meeting rooms are wanted, how many people should be planned for? Their size could simply be set to cater for the largest gathering that takes place, so that it never 'fails'. This is an extravagant approach if the big meetings only happen once a quarter, while considerably smaller ones take place weekly or daily. If meetings rooms are big enough only for small meetings, another space (say, a staff lounge) may need to be used, by arrangement, for that big quarterly meeting.

The amount of time over which particular activities take place should be included as part of the equation. Space needs to match the most typical extent of the activities, if it is to be used most cost-effectively, and must be used enough of the time to justify its provision. 'Utilization' is a useful concept. It describes how many people use the space in relation to its potential capacity and for what proportion of the available time. Use needs to be monitored in an existing situation and estimated for future changes to establish utilization rates:

% utilization =

$$\frac{\text{number of people using the space}}{\text{capacity}} \times \frac{\text{hours used}}{\text{hours available}} \times 100$$

In one organization a major conference and training facility and staff meeting rooms were carefully and regularly monitored. It transpired that most rooms had utilization rates of between 1 and 15 per cent. The most utilized room, the smoking room, had a 25 per cent utilization rate. These figures were surprising, even shocking, to the managers. On the basis of these data the company was able to replan the facilities to make better use of them over time. Some special needs may be so essential that, even though they occur only rarely, tailor-made space needs to be provided. It gets harder and harder to justify such uses, so examples no longer abound. The board room may be the last survivor.

Although organizations have more complex and subtle space requirements than they had a few decades ago, this does not mean that space-planning expertise is inevitably required. On the contrary: since what actually goes on in the office needs to be fully understood before a decision is made about how space should be divided up, the people in the organization are as important as outside experts. Advice may be required, but it need not be in the form of hiring an outside team to plan and execute a project. It may be available in the form of a brief consultation to enable in-house people to devise and implement suitable solutions. For a small organization one day of expert help, sorting priorities, devising a strategic approach and indicating particular strengths and weaknesses of current space use, may be all that is needed. Common sense can carry you a long way once you understand the possibilities inherent in buildings.

Summary

This chapter helps to address how much space should be given to each person and to each activity. It provides reasons for reducing the number of space standards to no more than three or four for most organizations.

How much space each person is worth needs to be determined. Space standards are used to answer this question. They are of great assistance both in estimating space requirements and in planning the use of space. An average lettable area per person of about 15 square metres is fairly typical for an ordinary office building in the UK, though in Scandinavian countries it is typically twice as much.

Individual space standards deal with the workplace 'footprint'. In the past standards have been defined by grade; the higher the grade the larger the space. So there have been few people at the largest standard and many at much lower allowances.

The trend is towards fewer standards, with less difference between them – a shallower pyramid. This allows for a more flexible approach to fitting floor layouts to an organization's needs and helps change to be more easily absorbed. Typical standards are now based more often on the amount of space needed for the job. Four or five different workstation layouts are likely to cover most needs in an organization. Six, 9 and 12 square metres are a good set on which to start to base a family of space standards. Modularity between space standards, so that they relate to each other, is likely to help in planning a building.

Space per person, as an average figure over an entire building, is an important measure. It can be used to relate the cost of a building to the people it houses. Density of occupation, a slightly different concept, is more relevant when applied to working areas. These measures must be re-evaluated in organizations where the population present in the building may vary from day to day and the places in which they work may vary depending on current tasks.

The importance of time as well as space has begun to be recognized. Priorities are established by how often a space is needed for a particular use as well as by how important that use actually is.

4 Four Walls and a Door – or I Want to be Alone

The new open plan office had worked its special magic on Janet's cheery disposition.

> *Monica, who worked in Personnel, took me from the plastic mahogany and subdued lighting of the executive floor to the metal desks and neon operations (Settlements) two floors below. About 30 people sat at metal desks, shuffling and ticking and passing and sorting piles of paper. Some of them gazed into computer screens as if they were crystal balls. No one seemed to be speaking but it was noisy and confusing ... We went through a pair of fire doors into another large office (Accounts). This one was divided up by freestanding partitions into a complicated maze, like a puzzle where you have to get a silver ball to the middle. The partitions were covered in a fuzzy brown material, repulsive to the touch, to deaden sound. I speculated that the work flow in Settlements was conducive to a completely open office layout while Accounts required small isolated units. Then why did disembodied hands rise above the furry walls with files and papers, why did disembodied heads peep round the sides?*
>
> John Mole, *Brits at Work*, pp. 16–17.

John Mole's evocative description of this first office in which he, an ex-senior manager turned writer, decided to find out what employment in the ranks was like indicates clearly that there are various layers of privacy, different types of enclosure. People can be located on separate floors – the bosses are often at the top of the building – or they may be in separate rooms, or merely screened from each other by 'partitions ... covered in fuzzy brown material' or, of course, not separated at all. In many organizations it is assumed that seniority brings with it a right to privacy and a luxurious environment. Junior status suggests being in the open.

Why is there so much open plan these days? Who gets an enclosed office? Does this reflect more than status? How far is enclosure or openness a necessary part of the way in which work is carried out? Or are they determined by other considerations? Should the use of enclosure take account of the way work is currently carried out, or of how you would prefer work to be carried out, or of space costs? Does the layout of a suite of offices influence the behaviour of the occupants? Are changes easy to bring about? And what happens if you try?

Work organization and buildings

The debate about open plan office buildings, where large groups occupy big spaces, versus highly cellularized ones, where many or most people have individual rooms, could take place only once office buildings existed that could be planned to accommodate large groups. When masonry load-bearing walls and timber ceiling joists were the form of construction used, only small rooms were possible. They were hard to change and encouraged static arrangements. They generally provided natural light and ventilation in each room, because of the small dimensions of the rooms. New building technologies changed all this. Steel for columns, joists and trusses, and then reinforced concrete frames, liberated space, which might or might not be divided up by lightweight partitions. Rooms could be any size, *and there was no need to have rooms at all.* Buildings could be deep in plan if light and air could reach where they were needed. Walls made of glass, and electricity, take care of the light. Fans and duct-work push air into the middle of deep space.

So now buildings can be provided to suit a variety of office-work organizations. Different proportions of open to enclosed areas, areas of different sizes, especially very large ones, have become possible. Long, thin buildings, about 12–15 metres wide, have a large perimeter in relation to their area, so cellular offices are easily planned without necessarily depriving other working areas of light and air. In such buildings the main complaints are dismal, narrow corridors, and that people never see each other.

Big, square buildings make large, open areas possible. Good light can be a problem, and ventilation a worse one – one that air conditioning has failed to solve in many cases (see chapter 6). The development of large, open plan, 'landscaped' office floors, the *Bürolandschaft* approach, with non-orthogonal furniture layouts and plenty of plants to soothe the eye and subtly subdivide the space, was promoted in Germany by the articulate, persuasive Quickborner team of designers in the 1950s. Privacy, particularly for the lower echelons of management and professional staff, was sacrificed to better communication between individuals and groups. Interaction was planned for, placing close together groups with a frequent need to contact each other. Only the most senior people kept their offices. It was recognized that if many offices were placed around the window walls, serving a fairly small proportion of the building population, the majority would be seriously disadvantaged, deprived of natural daylight, of views and of any possibility of fresh air. Large-scale openness was hailed as a way to bring a sense of contact with the outside to as many people as possible. The alternative approach, putting the offices in the middle, away from the windows, is possible but rarely popular with bosses.

Other approaches to enclosure have been developed to express the right balance between hierarchy and privacy in different organizations. Private space for concentrated work, allied to shared areas to bring about communication, results in the Swedish 'Combi' office. This is popular in northern Europe, though it has not caught on in North America or the UK. It uses a very large average amount of space, about 35 square metres of lettable area per person, which tempers its popularity where space is costly. The widely admired SAS building in Stockholm represents a version of this new prototype for an office building. It gives a private office to each person for concentrated work and small group spaces for teams of about twenty-four people. It also creates a large and beautiful covered street linking parts of the building and providing many opportunities for interaction.

Open plan versus cellular offices

Once choice is available, decisions, however tricky, need to be made, and there are more factors to be considered than the physical possibilities of the building. Privacy may be desirable; solitude can be a problem. Ample individual space may be pleasant; the cost may be prohibitive. The tension between satisfaction for the company and personal dissatisfaction is a key issue to be resolved.

Much discussion of the merits of open plan versus enclosed offices takes place among designers. Few management books discuss this in depth, although many tacitly assume that a manager has a private office. The basis for the decision about how much a building should be subdivided into separate offices is related to organizational culture and need. Different design approaches have been developed, seeking to fit the organizational needs to the amount and type of separation.

A simplified analysis of organizations can enable spatial organization to be seen as a reflection of the business organization. Where there is a

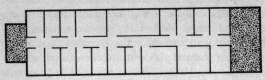

Long and thin – all cellular offices

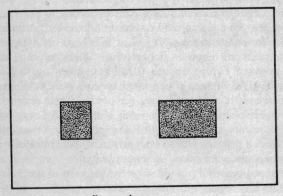

Big and square – all open plan

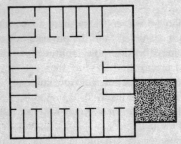

Combi office – everyone in cellular office PLUS shared space in open plan

Figure 4.1   Three types of building: long and thin, big and square and a Combi office.

great degree of hierarchy, status is marked out by spatial devices, size and subdivision, so that senior people have enclosed offices, and the more senior they are, the larger these offices. By contrast, the juniors are accommodated in open areas. Walls can inhibit communication. Where there is little need for communication, or where it may be damaging because of breach of privacy or loss of concentration, there is subdivision into single-person offices. This is the situation in most solicitors' offices. Where the need for interaction is urgent and the benefits of communication are great, as in the media industry, in advertising or in a creative design office, there are few spatial divisions. These relationships assume that buildings are responsive to the types or pressure described, that organizational culture creates spatial character. Though this can and does happen, it is fallacious to assume the reverse, that spatial reorganization will, of itself, bring about organizational rebirth.

A variety of factors influences choices about enclosure. The benefits of one approach rather than another are not always simple to evaluate, but some insights can be achieved by considering other building types. Take hospital buildings again. They demonstrate some of the reasons for, and effects of, enclosure. You are given an enclosed room if you are critically ill, or if your condition needs isolation, or if you can afford one and would prefer it. In the Nightingale ward beds in rows in a larger room are screened from each other by curtains. In some hospital designs small rooms, for between two and six people, are used. These design options have followed changes in the philosophy of how patients should be cared for. Boarding schools have moved away from large dormitories to single or two-person study bedrooms. Monasteries, which supplied the model for, and the origin of, boarding schools, vary according to the rules of behaviour of the order. A silent order provides cells for solitary meditation rather than a shared dormitory. Hotels offer, at a range of prices, many grades and sizes of individual rooms, with the option to include an extra family member for a marginal extra cost. Youth hostels, on the other hand, accommodate people of limited resources by offering dormitories, frequently with bunk beds.

Open plan for office design is no longer a new idea. Many accept it as inevitable. But an open, exposed expanse of office floor is far from universally popular with the majority stranded out there on the plain. Furniture manufacturers have responded with system furniture, particularly in North America, where many modern buildings provide the large-scale spaces suitable for landscaped offices. In the case of system furniture desks, storage and dividing screens come with rules, like those for a child's construction toy, so that they fit together to create individual workstations. One of the resulting layouts, the 'bull-pen' office, provides an approximate, though debased, version of cellularization within the open area and creates John Mole's maze in the Accounts Department, at a high furniture cost but a low building cost. This can have interesting tax effects on the difference between capital and revenue expenditure if the furniture is leased, not bought. Accountants have invested many happy hours of calculation in refining this calculation.

Open plan brings with it benefits as well as problems. Where the benefits are clearly perceived by all affected, where senior managers show by their actions that they are as committed as they expect their juniors to be, where everyone is willing to learn to adapt, it can be well justified. Such conditions for success are by no means easy to achieve. Where they are ignored or forgotten over time, the difficulties most complained about become significant. Some of these are discussed below. Newer ideas about the effects of open plan offices are also being considered by designers and social analysts. Where people have a disturbing impact on each other, this may intensify their reduced sense of control over their environment. A sense of control appears to be of importance and is being examined by researchers looking at sick building syndrome (see chapter 6). Providing environmental control for individuals in open plan is cumbersome and expensive. When twenty lights are controlled by a single switch there is no way for individuals to control the one light affecting their workplace. By contrast, a light switch for an enclosed room is simple to provide and is also easy to switch off – it is by the door as you leave the room, so it is an efficient, simple, energy-saving device. There are real design as well as management problems to be solved for offices where the decision for cost, for communication or for functional reasons is to provide open plan working areas for large numbers of staff. Layout, type and placement of such partitions as are required, the height of screens between desks where these are used and light switching devices are all important design issues.

What does it cost?

One reason for the spread of open plan office buildings is that this type of accommodation costs less per square metre to install, maintain and replan, and you need less of it for a given number of staff. Each of the different office plans in figure 4.1 can be viewed as a diagram showing how the relative importance of bureaucracy and interaction in an organization has been communicated to a design team. As far as the 'bottom line' is concerned, they each have space-per-person and fitting-out implications that have a significant impact on cost. Added costs are entailed by partitions, doors and their ironmongery and individually controlled lighting and heating, and waste is involved in finishes for smaller spaces. Though important, fitting-out costs have less impact than space-per-person costs, which recur annually.

The average amount of space per person depends in part on the level of enclosure. In open plan a desk can occupy 5 square metres of open space. In cellular arrangements the individual's desk must be replaced by at least 9 square metres, a minimal room. This increases the average space per person. The Combi office has an even higher allocation of space per person because shared areas for a group are added. Total space requirements for an organization are built up as shown in figure 2.2. The average space per person for a hypothetical group, based on the workplace standards illustrated in figure 3.3 and including primary circulation, varies with different arrangements. With more individual or small-group rooms primary circulation routes increase in length and hence in area. The average lettable space per person in open plan is about 7 square metres; for group offices for six people it rises to about 8 square metres, and for two-person offices to nearly 9 square metres per person. Where everyone has their own office it goes up to about 13 square metres per person, and in an arrangement like a Combi office it rises to 16 square metres per person, for this hypothetical group.

A need to contain the cost of space should not dictate the type of office plan, the degree of enclosure, chosen to support your business. Neither should it be ignored as an issue. The costs locked up in the space equation can be affected in several ways; limiting the amount of enclosure is only one. Omitting partitions makes less saving than seeking competitively priced furniture and finishes. It could cost 25 to 30 per cent more to fit out space to a similar standard for cellular space than for open plan, whereas costs could double between a 'basic' provision and a 'high-quality' one. Adopting new ways of working, and thus sharing space in different ways, may be more economic. Location decisions may be changed. A central, expensive location may be less important than lots of space and high levels of enclosure. Unless, of course, you can afford both space and place, now and in the anticipated future.

Change, churn and communication

Modern organizations must be fleet of foot if they are to survive. Change is the watchword, so churn must follow. Open plan space needs minimal reorganization. It easily accepts newly constituted groups, especially if a limited number of dimensionally related space standards, as described in the last chapter, are used. This may be a very good reason for adopting it but not necessarily the decisive one. Communication may be more important. Both should be taken into account. In times of rapid change, when new organizational structures are being implemented and frequently modified, the locations where people work in a building change. Mergers and growth in boom periods are followed by 'down-sizing' and streamlining in recessions. Team structures and members are constantly on the move. The newest management twist, 're-engineering', will undoubtedly lead to moves of individuals and groups as the entire way in which organizations work is subjected to radical change.

Fundamental space-planning policies, decisions about how much enclosure is required, have a major contribution to make. The less specific the subdivision of the space is to the particular group sizes that obtain at any time, the fewer partitions have to be moved to relocate differently structured groups. Fewer changes mean less cost and disruption. Moving partitions is disruptive at any time. In some buildings it is worse than others. In a city building, the London HQ of a major oil-exploration company, a plan was put forward to reorganize an area, move a partition and allow a stranded secretary to work more closely with her group. Engineers calculated that, as a consequence, the location of an air-conditioning unit would have to be changed, and the cost would be £8,000. Even making an opening in the partition for visual links would 'unbalance' the system. The change was vetoed. The building, through the design of its partition layout and air-conditioning system, dictated a work pattern that the manager and his group knew would be less productive, not to mention less pleasant for the secretary.

Open plan can aid communication and interaction. Management gurus stress the importance of new communication patterns, the prominence of team work, the liberating effects of new technology. The possibility must at least be considered that a manager behind his own office door, even when he says it is an 'open' door, is less likely to anticipate and adapt to the ever more ambiguous and fast-changing world. Office walls are themselves a form of insulation, if not against seeing the need for others to change, still often against having to change oneself. For a team to work together its members must be in communication. One simple way to achieve this is for all the members of the team to share a work room or space that helps to foster communication. The landscaped office was promoted on the assumption that increased interaction would result from its use.

Researchers have begun to look at communication in more detail.

Rather than simple openness, high levels of interaction seem to be encouraged in locations where lines of sight and access routes on the office floor link many workplaces. A topology that allows this is not always open plan. Equally some open plan layouts are such that this aim is not achieved. For organizations on several floors, interaction can be enhanced if the routes between floors are simple and as short as possible, with few direction changes. This idea is based on evaluating whether people are likely to interact with each other as they walk about in specific layouts, rather than assuming openness creates interaction.

The people serving in newly re-engineered organizations are less likely to be described as middle managers, but are more likely to be given considerable autonomy and responsibility for their own actions. Yet the reward for taking on responsibility is not an office of their own, as it might well have been when middle managers were in fashion. In the interests of improved teamwork these new-style workers may have had to give up the offices they once occupied, or at least forgo any expectation of promotion to an office.

Does it work? Are the benefits worth the deprivation? Where interaction is desired, it is often achieved in open plan. Freely offered comment from office workers questioned about their office building suggests that the theory that open plan aids team work and communication is borne out in practice, though there are also penalites.

'I prefer the open plan system. It is easier to be close to staff that you deal with on a regular basis. You are able to keep in touch with what is happening.'

'Togetherness creates team spirit. The major benefit of this office is the mixing of staff due to the open plan arrangement. The drawback is the noise level when concentration on work is necessary.'

Questionnaire responses: staff in offices that had changed to open plan from group rooms

---

Group rooms

The choice may not be between a personal private office or a perch in a battery hen-house. The number of people occupying a single space that is required to make an office open plan is not precisely defined in a dictionary. Between two and four people in a room hardly seems to justify the term open plan, but it seems reasonable to consider a room with around ten people as an open plan office. There are ways of laying out even a group of this size so that people are clustered in smaller numbers, though the whole area may still be, in effect, open plan. People in a large survey were asked to state with how many people they shared their room. They sometimes opted for the size of a small local group within a larger space rather than indicating that the area where they worked was essentially open plan. They may have suffered from some of the disadvantages of open plan, but their perception was that they were in a small area, usually accommodating three or four people.

A group room or a shared room, containing about four people, has several of the prized attributes of a personal office. Every occupant is close to a window, and the noise and disturbance to which they are subjected is from a small, defined group. The group can reach agreement about acceptable telephone voices, at-the-desk meetings or other sources of distraction. Conversely, it can sometimes be hard to ignore completely the conversation of a few colleagues, whereas the general noise level in a large open plan area is able to mask individual conversations. In a group room people can agree whether the window should be open, the lights on or the blinds closed. The distraction caused by the movement of people around the office as a whole is muted by the door. Rooms for small groups are common in office buildings. They are congenial in many respects, but from a layout and management point of view they have some of the disadvantages of single-person offices in cost with respect to both capital and replanning costs. They have a particularly rigidifying effect, making it hard to create new groups, dissolve them and bring them together in different forms, an aim that is important to the way modern companies work. If the room prescribes the size of group, say four or five people, because additional desks simply cannot be fitted in, this can be even more difficult to overcome than creating good working teams of varying sizes out of people in individual or two-person offices.

I NEED my own office

Q: **What can reduce grown men to tears?**
A: Having to give up their own office.
'Space is the most emotional thing in the whole of the company . . . Half the power base is having an office.'

Interview comment prior to the piloting of a changed office layout

A Room with a View, The L-shaped Room: these are not books about offices, but their titles convey the notion that a room can evoke strong feelings and be important for generating a sense of identity, security and role. The reasons given by those working in their own offices for continuing in solitary splendour are pretty consistent: seniority, confidentiality, concentration and the need to hold meetings. The assumption that seniority confers a right to an enclosed office is not made explicit. There is tacit recognition that in times of change this may be a weak argument, though in reality it is often a strongly held view. Personnel officers say that privacy is essential to allow private matters to be discussed with staff. Lawyers claim client confidentiality. Academics and editors want isolation for concentration and walls for books and paper storage. They forget that space is not a free good. Senior executives assume that company strategy must be a matter for security. Statements made in defence of retaining personal offices would imply that most telephone calls, however innocently they start, end up discussing matters that would be dynamite if they leaked out, that most one-to-one conversations with subordinates end in tears and that the constantly frustrated goal of most office dwellers is to get their heads down to write or calculate in uninterrupted creative silence. Not to mention the fact that they also need to hold private meetings in their offices.

Of course all these things take place. What is hard to learn is the truth about how often they happen, how unpredictable they are and whether, if known about in advance, they should or at least could take place in an enclosed room that is not a personal office. When pressed, people who 'need' their own offices may admit that unexpected developments during telephone conversations that result in a need for the highest discretion are not a daily, perhaps not even a weekly, occurrence. Most of the interviews that will end in tears can be predicted. Many people actually do their most creative work at home or on the train anyway. When a few colleagues are gathered together in a meeting they are, of course, only using one private office for the purpose, so the others are empty. In strictly functional terms, much work could take place somewhere other than in an enclosed personal office.

Status, tradition and identity also influence the desire for an office. Considerable persuasion may be required to alter entrenched views. Consider a hypothetical discussion between the chief executive of J. Robinson Foods and his finance director, recently hired from an organization that has benefited from more open planning.

J. Robinson III: My father had this office, all my friends have large offices and I don't see why I can't have one too.

Finance director: Let's look at the reasons why a chief executive might need a lavish office. First, for *status*, to protect his image in the eyes of the outside world and those in his organization. Second, because he may have many large *meetings*, either with his own staff or with senior managers from other companies, and he wishes to entertain them in his own office. Third, because space and *quiet* might be necessary for his work. Fourth, because matters he deals with may be *confidential*.

But let us also consider why he might not have one. First, it is expensive; the company may not be able to afford it, and such waste may create a bad impression. Second, it sets a precedent; all of his staff may aspire to offices of their own and feel aggrieved if they do not have one. Third, large meetings happen infrequently; most of the time the office contains only one person. Fourth, chief executives tend to travel a great deal to meetings elsewhere. Fifth, when they hold their meetings in their own offices they are interrupted by their staff giving them messages or asking them to sign documents or answer urgent calls. An individual large office is not necessarily the right solution.

J. Robinson III: I accept your points, but I still want my own office . . . because . . . well, because I *want* my own office.

Finance director: You talk like most senior managers. But in some organizations they have been asked to rethink their need for large offices. Let me tell you what some of them say after relinquishing them. They say that they communicate better with staff. They say that they understand far more about the workings of their organization. They say that they need fewer meetings, and

	those they have are shorter because they already know what is going on. They say that they feel part of a team instead of being isolated at the top.
J. Robinson III:	But surely they feel they have given up something very important?
Finance director:	They admit that sometimes they miss the splendid isolation of their lost offices, that sometimes they cannot concentrate properly on their work because of the distractions, that they may have lost some of their air of authority. The ones who seem most satisfied are those who instead have created a series of conference and entertainment rooms, available when they need them, used by others when they do not, rooms of beauty and on a generous scale, which are tidier and more dignified than their own messy offices. There they can talk to guests and staff when occasion demands. Some have kept an office just big enough for solo work or for meetings with one or two others. Give me a chance to show you that your authority will not be diminished, and your productivity may even be increased, by a different attitude to offices.
J. Robinson III:	You speak persuasively. Perhaps we can think again about the number, size and type of offices. I might be able to manage without one, or anyway with only a small one.

Some people do need an office, if not an ultra-lavish one, and this can apply even in an organization committed to open plan. As suggested by J. Robinson's finance director, status, meetings, quiet and confidentiality are all valid reasons in the right circumstances. There may well be people whose need for enclosure really *is* a reflection of status that should be emphasized and must be provided for. Others have a genuine need for frequent meetings, attended by several people, that would be disturbing if held in the open plan, and there may not be meeting rooms available. Quiet concentration may be essential for large parts of the day – academics are a case in point. Such people are often surrounded by more papers and reference material than normal and need wall space against which they can be stored. The most senior people in an organization – the governor of the National Bank, for instance – may deal with genuinely confidential material on computers or paper that is hard to keep 'for your eyes only' during a normal office day unless separation can be preserved by walls and a door. Some people depend on being able to reassure clients or informants to whom they speak on the telephone that conversations are fully confidential. Lawyers are frequently cited as an obvious group, although there are examples of shared rooms, and even shared desks, for legal professionals, so merely being a partner in a large law firm need not be an automatic passport to an office of one's own.

Where should the cellular office be located if it is used? How should a manager's office relate to the workplaces occupied by the team? It is common, especially in North American buildings, for individual offices to occupy the window walls, enclosing a group of junior staff and secretaries in the dark middle of the building. This is a poor environmental solution, though the team's location in relation to managers may be good. In some organizations the principle has been reversed, so that managers occupy the artificially lit interior and their staff are near the windows. The justification for this is that the senior staff have the benefit of more space and are less often at their desks. Another arrangement designed to place managers next to their teams results in a scatter of offices along window walls. If carefully planned these offices may give the additional benefit of screening small sections of open space from each other.

Where their relationship with each other is very important several managers can be grouped together, even if it places some of them away from their teams. At the most extreme is the top floor syndrome, where the directors inhabit a stratospheric area, far above the masses, surrounded by conference facilities, executive dining rooms and original works of art. In a prominent headquarters of a San Francisco bank the windows on that elevated floor are cleaned twice as often as those below. This way of allocating space is not so common as it once was, but it is useful where relationships between top managers and the outside world, as well as with each other, are paramount.

The trauma of change

Maybe J. Robinson III followed his finance director's advice. Maybe not. Whatever the rights and wrongs of open plan working areas, people usually feel that they are suffering if asked to change from enclosed offices to open plan. Even those who formerly shared with two or three other people can resent a move to larger open plan rooms. The trauma of change is not mentioned when the change is in the opposite direction. When staff previously in open plan are given offices of their own, stories are not heard of their suffering from isolation or their grief for companions they once enjoyed. So one must accept that there are real problems to be dealt with in the move to open plan.

Serious attention must be given to ensuring that people are not made to feel that they are being demoted by a change to open plan. The loss of an enclosed office happens naturally when a senior member of staff in a regional office is recruited to the central headquarters – rather like moving from the top of the primary to the bottom of the secondary school. Acclimatization can be difficult, but resentment is not usually a central reaction. A change from an enclosed office to large open plan spaces is less well accepted by existing job holders if it is not shared by senior staff. It is hard to accept that loss of an office is not equivalent to loss of status if there are others whose seniority apparently entitles them to an office. The more general the change, the more levels in the organization it affects, the less likely it is to give anyone a sense of personal inferiority.

Where the most senior manager can accept open plan working, adapt to the fact of being potentially under scrutiny at all times and maintain a managerial role without the support of clear spatial definition, it is easier for others to acknowledge that their own worth is not in question. Where senior people indicate the value to be gained from the openness, encourage the interaction between hitherto separate groups and functions and lead the change from in front, its benefits will be maximized and will help to cushion the trauma of change. Bosses who take the lead and embrace the change personally can have a powerful psychological effect. Senior managers who go open plan at the same time as all the rest of the staff are on higher moral ground – important in a situation with such significant psychological dimension. In a practical sense, they are also more likely to make sure that the disadvantages are minimized and the bugs in the planning ironed out, as they are affected personally by the success or failure of the way the open area functions.

An emotion that can only be described as bitterness is still aroused when people who expected to be given an office of their own upon reaching a particular level in the organization see that privilege disappear just before, or just after, attaining that status, regardless of how many others suffer the same change. Here the gap between expectation, which may have played a strong motivational role, and reality is like waking up and realizing that something pleasant was actually only a dream. It is an emotional rather than a functional shock.

For some, however, there are functional problems as well: those whose work habits are based on the availability of a personal office. There is the loud-telephone-voice habit, which does not move easily into open plan. There is the occupant who is proud to be able to navigate unerringly through the layer of papers, several months deep, on every available surface in the room. This is a form of 'horizontal' filing for which open plan cannot offer sufficient space or clearly defined boundaries, even if the squalor can be tolerated. Then there is the smoker, who has no one else's feelings to consider and can smoke when in an enclosed office but will be outvoted in the open plan and deprived of access to the addiction except in a smoking room full of strangers and probably on another floor. These are real difficulties for which there are no easy solutions. Each group of people has different causes for concern, and each case deserves thought about how to overcome the problems. Some people are very hostile to change, even when the change is soundly based. They can cause an atmosphere that makes the change harder for everyone, even for those people who thought they would benefit from it. Such people need individual consideration, which must take the form of helping them to adapt without reducing their ability to function rather than adapting the proposed change to suit them at expense of others or of the office function as a whole.

Giving something back in exchange

There is some scope for compensation, when open plan is introduced, involving the office building and how it is planned and managed. The environment can be made attractive with plants, artwork and good lighting. Efficient new furniture can be offered. Other amenities may be provided for which there was previously no space (see chapter 7). Portable computers, mobile phones and the opportunity to work a more flexible day or week may help to soften the blow. Some organizations have taken very seriously the need to make better use of their space and to promote better communication within the office. They have decided to place all staff, even the most senior managers, in open plan as a matter of principle. When this disrupted a long tradition of hierarchy, compensation was needed, and some of the above measures have been successfully adopted. For others engaged in creative design or media activities the benefits of interaction have always been appreciated, and even the MD has always worked in the open. These organizations have generally learned to make excellent use of shared meeting and interview rooms for the times when people need to be private.

The provision of alternative enclosed rooms, if people, especially managers, cease to have enclosed offices, must be carefully considered. As well as rooms needed for meetings, conveniently located near the working areas, there may be a need for interview rooms, to be used during recruiting sessions or staff reviews. Whether designated specifically as interview rooms or not, these can be located near the personnel or human resources team, who have frequent need for such spaces. The amount of time spent in meetings in their own offices is exaggerated by many managers. Surveys in a wide range of organizations have shown that in situations where about 10 per cent of the staff have enclosed offices, meetings in them take up only about 15 per cent of the working day. None the less, if everyone were in open-plan, even this level of use would require several dedicated meeting rooms to allow for overlaping schedules. Meeting rooms may be grouped in a suite to which several teams within the organization have access. Flexibility can be added by folding doors, though for good ones that are adequately sound-proof and do not look temporary you must expect to spend a considerable amount. A suite of rooms, especially if they are to be used primarily for meetings with people from outside the organization, can be placed near reception to avoid the disturbance and security risk of outsiders entering the main working part of the office. They can be serviced efficiently, for coffee and even meals, if they are located near the kitchens or have a local serving pantry. Shared quiet rooms or library and reference areas may be provided to satisfy the need for separation and quiet, and these may be even better suited to total concentration than enclosed offices, where people can telephone or drop in.

Control noise and distraction

'A total open plan system is not conducive to concentration. This needs urgent action. The noise at times is appalling. Interruptions are frequent and unnecessary.'

'The office can be noisy for telephone calls due to open plan.'

'The open plan concept has failed. People feel cramped for space, and the noise levels cause constant distractions.'

Questionnaire responses: staff who had changed to open plan from group rooms

> *'Open plan is like trying to have a pee in an open field. There's nowhere to hide'*
>
> Interview with open plan office occupant

Status-related issues and individual functional idiosyncrasies are only part of the problem of open plan environments. A perennial complaint is that the noise created by others on the telephone or in conversation with people at their desks, and the distracting effect of seeing people move around, prevent concentrated work. This is, to some extent, always going to present difficulties. Soft surfaces, carpets, upholstered chairs and fabric-covered screens can all help to reduce sound levels. A very thick carpet, laid over a very thick underlay, can reduce ambient sound by as much as 70 per cent. Many carpets in offices do not reach this standard, and even where they do, a 70 per cent reduction in noise can still leave a very distracting residue. Screens that are described as acoustically efficient should absorb 85 per cent of the sound hitting them. Again, this seems an impressive figure, but most of the sound that causes disturbance will not actually hit the screen; it will go over or bounce around. But no sound deadening or introduction of 'white' noise – an indistinguishable background sound intended to cover and disguise sharper, random sounds – wholly prevents the hyper-sensitive from being disturbed by the noise made by their colleagues, particularly if they are pre-disposed to be disturbed because of their dislike of the open plan arrangement. The distance between people is important, so the area allocated to each person, the density of occupation, affects how disturbing someone else's conversation may be. Whether they are facing each other is even more significant, so if the people are within 2 or 3 metres of each other, positioning their desks at 90° to each other may help reduce the problem.

Movement catches the eye, and people passing by do easily distract. If desks are placed so the occupants face a busy corridor or a centre of activity such as a photocopier, their work may suffer. The value of being able to hear what others are saying, to be aware of developments, to make unplanned contributions, to know who is doing what is part of what the improved communications of the open plan is about. This should not be taken to mean that the distractions are all productive and must be tolerated uncritically. They need to be understood and controlled, in just the way that time-and-motion studies sought understanding and control of fragmented production processes.

It is a new management task to observe and understand the dynamics of whatever degree of openness is deemed best suited to the activities being carried out in order to get the best out of the benefits and control the disadvantages. Only with knowledge of what happens in different physical arrangements can sensible decisions be made. It seems as if no thought had been given to the needs of Settlements and Accounts in John Mole's example but rather that decisions had been based on tradition and clout. Accounts were spiritually or habitually closer to the finance director and thus merited more subdivision, although in practice they did not want to be cut off by the 'fuzzy brown' screens. Careful thought during the space planning of an open area can greatly reduce the problem of distraction so that it is felt only by those who so dislike the concept of open plan that any distraction is an insult. Two types of input are needed to create successful open plan offices: first, design input to provide the correct layout, screens and quiet places of escape; second, management input to help people to use the space effectively and to feel comfortable in it. Much can be done to train people to be considerate – for example, to lower their voice when on the telephone, to sit down when talking to colleagues so that the sound does not travel so far, to turn the bell on the telephone to the quietest ring, to move to a 'quiet room' when concentration is essential. A clean desk policy, and good facilities management to ensure that tops of cupboards, spaces by firedoors, and corners under the desks do not fill up with surplus piles of paper, can be very effective in creating an attractive atmosphere.

In a government office that took the radical step of putting everyone, including the most senior manager who is in charge of 1,000 people, into open plan rules have been devised to ensure 'good open plan manners'. Any visitor who stops to ask a member of staff a quick question is automatically asked to sit down. This greatly reduces the disturbance of their chat.

Walls, partitions and screens

Four walls and a door make a room. There are usually at least a few enclosed offices. There are always some rooms with walls, even in organizations where even the most senior staff work in open plan, for such areas as meeting rooms, group rooms and stationery or computer rooms. There are several ways to build the separation. There are walls that are built on site, fixed and solid, whether timber or masonry. There are factory-made partitions, which may be constructed in a wide variety of ways but have a less solid look and may, indeed, be removable. The nearest equivalent in the open plan is screens reaching up to somewhere between desk and ceiling height.

As with all decisions, functional, financial and aesthetic considerations need to be borne in mind when making a choice of partition. This choice may be overt when planning and commissioning a new layout, or it may be tacit when deciding to move to an office building where a particular partition type has already been chosen and installed. The main issues are: should the partitions be permanently fixed and built solidly as part of the building or be movable to some degree? And should they be partially, completely or not at all glazed?

For confidentiality, sound deadening is important. Measurements of sound levels make use of a logarithmic scale, so that twice as much sound raises the noise level by only a few decibels. Control of sound has to take into account the frequencies of the sound, the noisiness of the location, the quietness desired, and the distances between the sound and the person to be protected. A reduction of about 40 decibels reduces adjacent conversation to an unobjectionable level on a fairly noisy site. The sound deadening offered by different types of partition needs to be reviewed. As sound travels, it leaks above suspended ceilings, below raised floors, through the cracks around apparently well-fitting doors and past poorly fitted partition systems. All things being equal, however, weight helps to reduce sound transmission. Solid walls, permanently fixed, are likely to be heavier than partition systems and may be cheaper to build in the first place. On the other hand, for an office layout that can be expected to change within a few months or a year or two lighter partitions that can be easily removed, and may also be relocatable, reduce the disruption and cost of such changes. For many organizations this consideration is far more important than achieving the highest level of sound deadening.

Glazing can be used to reduce the claustrophobic effects of corridors, to allow 'borrowed' light to reach interior spaces and to enhance communication when visual links are helpful – for instance, it allows people to see that the occupant is busy before bursting in. Some glazing may be required by fire regulations, although this may be as small as a porthole in a door. Larger areas of glass may be provided as panels in doors or partitions, or as full-height glass partitions. Blinds can act as screens when it is preferable for people not to be able to see into rooms. A current design fad is etched glass, which allows visual privacy without blocking light, though many types are easily marked when touched, and can look rather unkempt, as greasy marks are often hard to remove.

Screens, normally fabric-covered panels stopping short of the ceiling and separating one person from another, are the compromise eagerly grasped by those groups whose need for defined personal space cannot be met in truly open layouts. Beware of the free-standing screens that can be moved from place to place. Not only do they usually have feet which stick out to trip the unwary, but also the bullies, the self-important and the truly antisocial manage to acquire these as efficiently as magnets attract iron filings and create enclosures and empires quite irrelevant to the smooth working of the whole organization.

Screens connected to desks come in two distinct types. Some of them are essential to hold up the desk; others stand hard up against a desk that could support itself. The latter type may be needed to provide what is coyly known in the trade as a 'modesty panel', a low-level screen to stop the chaps staring at nylon-sheathed legs across the room. The bit that sticks up above the desk can be used or abused. It may function merely to stop papers dropping off the desk on to the floor. It may rescue people who work face to face from eye contact or from staring into the rear end of their opposite number's computer. Even if acoustically efficient, it may not prevent noise travelling, but then a good part of the distraction of someone else's conversation is being fully aware or what they are doing while they talk. A screen can act as a support from which to hang shelves and telephone stands or a surface on which to pin working material – say, maps of sales areas, administrative aids like telephone lists, or family photos and certificates of job achievement. Many types of screen can give you a bruised thumb if you try to stick in a drawing pin, so if they are really wanted as display surfaces, check that they are suitably constructed.

Different heights have different uses. As screens get higher, they cut out more and more light and air, so the pleasant expansive feeling that can be one of the benefits of open plan space is replaced by a gloomy maze – remember Mr Mole? Plan layouts of screens so that those parallel to the window wall are minimal in height, say around 300 mm (one foot) above the desk surface. Reduce to a minimum the number that are treated as a substitute for full-height partitions. They nearly always enclose an area that is smaller than it would be if it were a real room. In addition there is a danger that there may be several layers of screened workstations between the window and a circulation route, so the overall effect can easily become poky and confusing, the very opposite of the open plan, interactive environment. Sell any free-standing ones left over from the last office-planning exercise.

A move back to cellular offices?

The dislike, felt by many, of open plan, the feeling that it may alienate people at least as much as it allows them greater opportunities for communication, has fuelled active discussion of the possibility of returning to the older pattern of more highly cellularized buildings. In Europe cellular offices have been popular for some time. The influence of North America has been in the opposite direction. Although *Bürolandschaft*, free-flowing layouts and plenty of plants on vast office floors, is associated with Germany, the open plan office was really a big hit in America. North Americans have little experience of long, narrow buildings or ones with a maze of tiny rooms clustered around a honeycomb of light wells. The North American urban legacy has few old buildings constructed before big spans were possible, hence their office buildings are large and high, with lifts to carry people up twenty, then forty, then a hundred storeys, and readily suited to open plan. Much of the development capital that fuelled office-building booms in Britain after 1945 was influenced, even provided, by American companies. The style to which they had grown accustomed across the Atlantic was replicated, albeit not very lavishly. Recently the importance of international cooperation between European companies has become more significant. Other office cultures and ways of working have come to the notice of users and designers. There are, for example, rules in France about how far from a window your desk can be. This reduces the depth of buildings and immediately reduces the benefits of open plan. The Scandinavians, the French, the Dutch and the Germans show a preference for enclosed, cellular office planning. Since people in other countries would like this too, there is a possibility that more new buildings will be constructed on models that at least allow for a high level of cellularization, even if they do not demand it. There is still, however, a huge stock of office buildings, occupied or empty, that will not work well with a high percentage of cellularized space, so many people will be working in open plan for a long time to come, and care in fitting it out will be well repaid.

Summary

This chapter helps you to think through how much space should be allocated to enclosed private offices and how much should be open plan. It suggests approaches that may ease the transition to more open plan if that becomes the policy of the organization.

Enclosed offices were the norm until office buildings were built with minimal internal structural divisions. The prevalent assumption is that seniority confers a right to privacy even when construction enables everyone to be in the open plan. There are situations where enclosure is suitable and necessary. Open plan office floors have encouraged the development of system furniture, which is often used to give an illusion of enclosure.

Enclosed offices cost more to provide. The average space per person is larger and the capital and replanning cost is higher. Open plan facilitates change, making it easier as well as cheaper. It is often adopted in order to improve communications. Where the plan, however much or little openness it incorporates, enables direct visual and physical communication with large numbers of people, interaction is increased. For appropriate groups, the benefits that this brings are much appreciated.

Those whose status, expectations, habits of self-importance lead them to believe that they need their own office can be hard to convince. There are good arguments for adopting other solutions even among senior people, whose example will ease the disruptive and distressing effects of change for other staff.

The benefits of open plan are often jeopardized by noise and distraction. Awareness of this problem, careful layout planning, the introduction of special 'quiet' areas where justified, the use of sound-deadening finishes, white noise and staff training can all help.

Where enclosure must be provided there is a choice between full-height separation in the form of partitions or walls and lower division provided by screens. Different partition types have varied levels of permanence, but the heavier they are, the more efficiently they intercept sound. The spaces above and below ceilings and floors can allow sound to 'leak' if they are not carefully designed. Screens are least successful if they are treated as 'almost partitions'. Heights need to be controlled to allow light and openness to be enjoyed generally.

There is a belief that, as many people prefer enclosed offices and they are commonly provided in continental European countries, there will be a shift toward providing more buildings that may be highly cellularized. Meanwhile many existing buildings are not suitable for subdivision, so the planning and management of open plan space will be a valuable skill for some time to come.

5 A Desk and a Light are All I Need

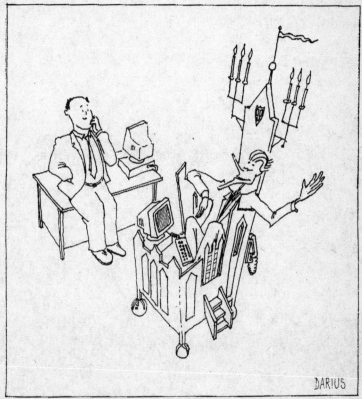

'Some of us would rather sacrifice comfort for style.'

> *The furniture looks very pretty but isn't functional. Many of the locks haven't worked since day one. Drawers do not fit properly and are constantly coming off runners. Chances are that in five years' time we will be left with a pile of rubble.*
>
> Questionnaire response in an office with new furniture

There are literally hundreds of companies making office furniture. Can they really all be making different things? More than 160 firms exhibited at a recent exhibition of chairs in London and each had several models on display. Very few chairs were for use in houses or hotels or for public places. Most were for office use, and they did not even include any of the ones that you kneel on, so fashionable as the ultimate solution to comfortable and healthy sitting a few short years ago. Although a few looked similar, there really were a lot of different shapes, and sizes, and qualities, and costs. Not only chairs come in a wide variety. Office furniture is big business. The UK market is around £500 million per year; competition is fierce, and the result is too much choice in a partially fashion-driven environment in which poor purchases are made as easily as good ones unless you know what you are doing. Do you have to depend on specialists in such a complicated world?

A desk is not just a desk

> [*For the executives*] *furniture tends to be of a higher quality than elsewhere in the organization . . .*
>
> Fritz Steele, 'The Ecology of Executive Teams: a New View of the Top'

People react to furniture as a symbol of many things; they do not merely take a rational view of how useful an item will be. Marketing information exploits this, as managers well know. Catalogues gloss over the useful information and provide images of a lifestyle. The boss gets rosewood; the open plan secretarial area gets a colour scheme suited to a spring collection of ladies' separates in a department store.

There are ways to bring order to chaos and isolate important information from the noise of marketing. The most common furniture items, used by nearly all office staff, are a desk, a chair and local storage units. Specialized items, like tables and chairs for meeting rooms, cashier points, dealing desks, bulk-storage systems are sometimes needed. They are important, often sophisticated and expensive, but do not, for most organizations, represent the main part of the furniture budget. Take stock first, therefore, of just the desk, the chair and local storage. This combination of items is known as a 'workstation'.

Several aesthetics are to be found. There are ethereal, slim, high-tech items which hover on a single supporting beam that is all-important structurally but hidden discreetly under the desk surface. There are elaborate workplaces carefully designed and coordinated with a place for everything, from trays for product literature, pens and company stationery to a hook for a coat and a bracket for the telephone. There are sturdy desks supported on metal or wooden legs or frames, which vary considerably in elegance. Do-it-yourself, self-assembly and bargain items, affordable but flimsy and short-lived, are another solution. Practical, cheap and without a claim to being furniture are desks made of a flush door balanced across two metal filing cabinets from a second-hand outlet dealing in bankrupt stock. Many furniture lines are based on a wooden construction, and the suppliers of the finest of these, such as Gordon Russell since the 1930s, have had the monopoly until recently in supplying chief executives' furniture. Utilitarian metal furniture was initially provided for the clerical masses and formed the basis of the business of say, Steelcase, the largest furniture supplier in the world. It has now been redesigned and increasingly come to be accepted as high-quality. There are workstations majoring on ergonomic adjustability with clever levers and ratchets or, in heavy-duty situations, motorized means of altering heights, angles or slopes to suit different users. Manufacturers laid particular stress on such capabilities during the period when the EC VDU directive was being developed in anticipation of a need for adjustability that has not fully materialized, since the obligatory adjustability can normally be provided by chairs. Refinements in manufacturing techniques have allowed for more 'interesting' shapes, so now the fashion is for curves, D-ends, 'tear-drops' and add-on meeting or computer spaces to replace rectilinear desks and for slim, bevelled edges to replace flat ones.

There are two general philosophies about how workstation furniture can be provided, represented by stand-alone and integrated systems. Some firms make single stand-alone items, perhaps only desks or cupboards or chairs. Others make versions of all three items so that an entire office building can be furnished fully with their products. Furniture standing in an environment provided by the building is the traditional end of the market. Then there are firms that manufacture system furniture. All the bits that make up the desk and local storage are ingeniously fixed together, with additional items like dividing screens, cable ways and task lighting, even perhaps local air-conditioning. (The office chair, thank goodness, is still separate and mobile, not the fixed cafeteria arrangement where you slide into a seat growing out of the table or bolted to the floor.) The furniture itself creates the environment that happens to be housed in the building. Herman Miller produced the first commercially successful system furniture, Action Office, in the 1960s. Since then the market has expanded enormously. In between these extremes there is a grey area, where bits blend into systems. Furniture designed to be assembled from a range of components, so that in different combinations a wide variety of end results can be achieved, is becoming more and more common. The accessories that go with the furniture, such as task lights, are optional.

The choice of a furniture system commits the user to continued use of the same system, so it must be one that serves its purpose and is liked by user groups. New items are restricted to the range supplied with the system, so unforeseen changes may be hard to deal with. On the other hand, the choice of unrelated items from the same or different suppliers makes coordination difficult. In aesthetic terms it is hard to create a sense of unity; in a practical sense the dimensions of different items may not fit well together, leaving little gaps or overlapping bits that are hard to clean and make for wasteful use of space. Component ranges can offer a compromise – unity without a full straitjacket, coordinated dimensions and style that do not allow the furniture to take over the whole environment. This type of furniture is not problem-free. In order to allow for choice, the components are often complex and over-specific and may involve keeping stocks of many different parts if the potential for flexibility is to be exploited.

In order to maximize flexibility consider a desk to which a *separate* 'return' can be added. When an L-shaped arrangement is created out of a single item, the return is fixed on one side, so that in different locations it may not be suitable. The alternative, to create the L shape with two separate items, must be balanced against the higher cost of two surfaces and the fact that a single item has the advantage of having no join or crack in the worktop. The choice depends in part on the extent to which future changes are likely to require revised desk layouts or to mean moving people rather than desks.

Quality and value for money are everyone's objectives. They may be achieved by either approach, although full system furniture is generally more expensive. This may be reasonable, as it aims to do more, creating a whole environment. It is often what people feel they need if they are familiar with the USA office environment and if they are in the process of being led, or driven, protesting from a highly cellular environment to a more open-plan one. Another effect is that it is far harder to modify, so that a level of visual and spatial organization is introduced that is less easily destroyed when numbers and functions change.

The furniture criticized in the quote at the start of the chapter had instant appeal because of its colour and finish, but the user, not a specialist in furniture choice, readily identified the main causes of problems that recur in some ranges. The joints are poorly designed and not robust; the locks are badly made; the cheerful glossy finishes do not make up for the structural deficiencies. One organization believed it was getting a bargain when it bought 1,000 desk pedestals at £5 each (rather than the normal £50–£150) from a furniture company that was going out of business. This was twice as many as it needed but it was felt that if there were a few duds in the batch, the low price would more than make up for the inconvenience of storing the surplus and redeploying it as required. The furniture manufacturer was going out of business for a reason. The pedestals were badly made, and at the rate at which they were literally falling apart the whole stock looked as though it would need replacement within a two-year period. So what with the initial cost, the problem of finding storage space for the surplus until it was used up, the irritation of those whose pedestals fell apart once, twice, and yet again, this was a very bad bargain indeed.

Standards for strength and safety with which manufacturers are expected to comply have been drafted by government bodies. Certificates can be requested of suppliers to prove that their products meet the necessary levels. In addition, simple common-sense checks can test most aspects of the suitability and sturdiness of furniture. If you sit heavily on the edge of the desk, does it feel as if it will collapse? Are the edges smooth, with neatly finished corners? Do desks placed side by side line up at the same level? Is it easy to pull off pieces that are supposed to be demountable – the covers of cable runs, fabric panels and edge trims? Is it easy to put them back again? Do the drawers open smoothly, and do their fittings feel robust? Do the file sizes that you use fit into them easily, with minimum wasted space? Do keys protrude so far that a passer-by will be snagged? The furniture supplier also needs to be checked. A guarantee that parts will be available for up to ten years to repair or add to the furniture is important. The turn-around time for additional orders needs to be agreed. The quality of the installation service must be checked against references. If special finishes have been offered, then continued availability without a penalty price must be established. Before a big order is placed, a factory visit may be warranted to see the quality of the supplier on home ground rather than in a showroom, where problems can more easily be disguised.

Storage

> *'People are like bloody squirrels – they keep everything they ever come across.'*
> Training manager of a large corporation

The storage story is possibly the most important aspect of furniture. There are rapid changes in what is being stored throughout the office and what is needed at the desk. Electronic storage is in its infancy but will certainly increase over the next decade. Meanwhile the storage of physical items continues to expand. Everyone keeps far more than they need and need what they have not got. Policies for storage must be worked out. How much paper is it reasonable for each member of staff to keep personally? Does your organization generate so many administrative forms, from staff-appraisal documentation to time and expenses sheets, that the company is paying time and again for creating, copying and filing such records? Should each person be offered space for spare shoes, handbags, personal mugs and coffee jars? Should everyone keep their own mini-stationery store at the desk? Whatever the policy is, you must seek out the right containers.

The most desirable desk may come from a manufacturer who has not given sufficient thought to storage requirements. Maximizing the use that can be made of the internal dimensions of an under-desk pedestal or a free-standing cupboard unit requires detailed attention to height and width. Finding the right storage furniture for different purposes is *never* simple. If many different requirements must be met, it can be almost impossible to find the perfect solution that allows some coordination of the items selected. As always, compromise may well be required. Books, files and folders, computer printout, computer tapes and disks are all pulled off a shelf using different movements, come in different sizes and are referred to in different ways. Consider the simple file. In the US both foolscap and quarto are in common use. In the UK the occasional foolscap file coexists with those for A4. A drawer designed for foolscap is too wide for A4 (or quarto), and the hanging frame in the drawer needs to be adjusted. This may mean that A4 files hang parallel to the sides, not the front of the drawer. Why should anyone complain about this? Because it is unfamiliar and, if it is also unexpected, may be the straw that breaks the camel's back during a period of change. Storage systems are normally built of either timber or steel. Timber filing units cannot compete with metal ones, which are often better designed, more space-efficient and more robustly built.

The capacity of different units varies considerably in relation to the space they occupy. A four-drawer filing cabinet, a common item of furniture, takes up more floor space for the volume of storage that it contains than a cupboard containing lateral files. The difference is partly in the different way the files are accessed. If a person is to pull out a drawer before leaning over to extract a file, the floor space needed must accommodate the cabinet, the open drawer and the user standing in front of the drawer. With a lateral filing unit the user stands in front of the cupboard to extract the file from a hanging pocket. Doors either stick out beside the person, in the same depth of space that the person occupies, or they may be the tambour type that rolls down the side and behind or up at the top. The space used is about two thirds that of the drawer unit. A further advantage of lateral files is that they can be in a taller unit than filing cabinets without toppling over and thus save even more floor area for the amount of material stored. To see which file to extract, it is not possible to look into a drawer whose top is above eye level, hence there are two-, three- and four-drawer cabinets but not five- and six-drawer ones. Lateral frames can go higher, typically to five or six levels, because it is possible to reach up to a shelf above your head to pull down a file as long as the label can be read.

The capacity of different storage units is shown in figure 5.1. The high-density types are suitable if large volumes of files need to be frequently and randomly accessed. The larger and heavier the equipment

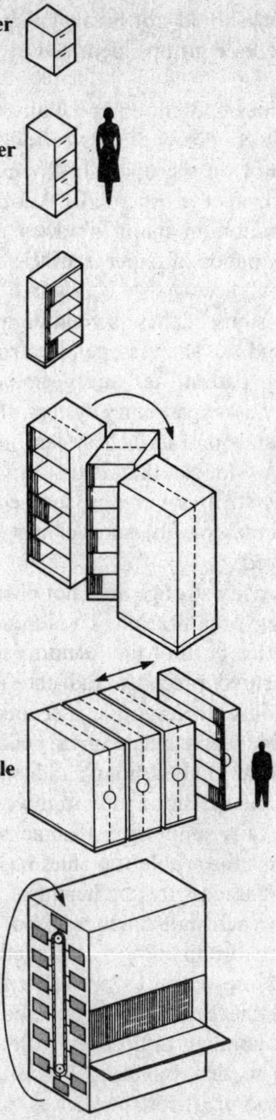

	Capacity, linear metres	Area* used, square metres	Linear metres per square metre
Two-drawer filing	1.2	0.75	1.6
Four-drawer filing	2.4	0.75	3.2
Cupboard four rows high	4.0	1.0	4.0
Revolving	10.5	1.75	6.0
Moving aisle	5.5	0.87	6.3
Power filing	52.7	3.25	16.0

*Area includes the storage unit and access to it

Figure 5.1 Capacity of different storage units.

being installed, the more care must be taken to ensure that its location will not need to be changed in future. It should be easily accessed from as many parts of the office as possible but should not break up space into arbitrary chunks based merely on the user groups identified at the planning stage.

An ingenious revolving storage unit, 'times two', doubles the amount of storage in each cupboard by placing a second row of shelves back to back with the first. If what you want is not on the open shelf, simply spin the shelf around and it will appear from the other side. Another system is rolling or sliding shelves, common in many libraries and increasingly used to control the growing mounds of paper in offices. Its efficiency comes from the fact that only one access aisle is required for many shelf units. The most up-market versions of these have a digipad on which you dial up the file you need, and the shelves open electronically, revealing the file. The power filing 'paternoster' units similarly allow a specific location to be called up by a keypad entry system, then the machine, electronically guided, moves around its belt system until the desired shelf is in front of the open slot so that items can be accessed. Manufacturers of these systems stress savings in staff costs because file retrieval is so efficient. Whether or not such claims are justified, space efficiency is certainly achieved.

Just because a unit is capable of high-density storage does not always mean that it will automatically benefit your organization. The essential issue with storage is that heights and widths, both of the furniture and the material to be stored, must be measured precisely and carefully related to each other. A specific area to house, for example, a reference archive may be occupied by tall shelf units nearly reaching the ceiling. Installing a mobile racking system could mean that, although additional runs of shelf units would fit in the space, the height of each unit would be reduced because of the height of the rails supporting the racks at floor level. The difference might mean that the whole top shelf has to be reduced in height by enough to make it useless for the height of the material in the archive. The lost shelf on each unit might well not be compensated for by the additional number of units. Poorly installed or badly balanced mobile units of any kind are prone to problems that never arise with fixed, static units. Even the British Library, used to dealing with book storage, has had to combat difficulties with the mobile racking ordered for the stacks in its new building. The length and height of the entire shelf units were too great for the shelves to be stable when moved. A slight 'wave' movement was enough to create the danger that books could be brushed off the shelf and then damaged by being squeezed between two units as they closed up. That items may drop off mobile units always has to be taken into account. With the revolving units, for example, if a file falls to the floor at the back of a unit there must be some space behind, and a way to access the space, if the file is to be retrieved. As in other situations, the more sophisticated and complex the object, the higher the cost and the more that can go wrong. These are the penalties that must be paid for the very real advantages such units can offer. Another point to remember is that to change from one type of unit to another takes time and effort. Converting from file drawers to lateral frames requires new file pockets and days spent relabelling everything, in short a clerical nightmare.

The mobile worker's unit

A new storage unit is now becoming available. Despite all the interest that has been shown in teleworking and the mobile workforce, the problem of how to provide for the storage requirements of the worker who is often not there has been tackled slowly. Without a desk of one's own there is no personal desk pedestal, no shelf or pinboard above the desk, nor is there a desktop on which to put photos of the family, a stapler, a pen tidy. An early furniture solution was to give each worker a mobile pedestal and exploit its mobility by storing it in a pedestal 'parking lot', allowing its owner to wheel it to a desk when in the office. This has usually, though not invariably, been found to be unsatisfactory. Pedestals are not particularly easy to move when loaded full of files – in fact, they are an ergonomic disaster as far as daily mobility is concerned. They are often not large enough, and they take up as much floor space as would a taller unit of greater capacity. They also have a tendency to be left around the office instead of being returned to their parking space, and then they get moved out of the way by an exasperated colleague. When people return to the office they have to spend time searching for their own units.

One of the first organizations to follow up the new possibilities of work away from the office is IBM UK. Working with the furniture company that has supplied much of their furniture over recent years, they specified and prototyped a unit, somewhat like a personal locker, that would serve this mobile population. Other furniture manufacturers are beginning to respond similarly, usually urged on by clients. An independent stationary unit taller than a mobile pedestal for each person, lockable if required, with a range of interior fittings, is being marketed. The fittings do the job that would traditionally have been done by parts of a desk. Some are similar to those you would find in a desk pedestal, such as a pen tray or a filing frame; some might be on top of a desk, such as in and out trays or a shelf for files and reference books. Sometimes the door has a mail slot or carries a pin space or a frame for family photos or the sales record diploma. A large basket or container for carrying files to the desk can be designed into the unit. And the unit carries a neat label to say to whom it belongs. This latter refinement is sadly usually missing on all storage units but should always be requested, as it takes only a few months for a new set of cupboards to be covered with torn sticky labels, Blu-Tacked sheets of paper or post-it-notes identifying owners and contents.

Health and safety law requires you to replace the furniture – or does it?

The existence of back pain is not disputed, though its causes and prevention are debated. Repetitive Strain Injury (RSI) is not accepted as a real condition by some, although some sufferers claim to be able to work no longer. Regulations attempt to limit the problems encountered by office workers as a result of the ergonomics of their furniture and equipment. People vary greatly in their physical dimensions. The task of the furniture industry, in attempting to meet the ergonomic needs of all users, is not simple. Health and safety regulations for the workplaces of people who use VDUs have been hammered out in the EC and enacted in the UK since 1993. They give guidance on the performance of desks, chairs and the VDUs themselves. When a new project is undertaken, a new building built, these requirements are liable to be checked. Any new furniture must comply with the new regulations. All organizations must replace non-compliant furniture by 1996.

The furniture industry is trying hard to exploit this. By reassuring potential purchasers that their furniture meets all the requirements, they imply that much existing furniture probably does not. Whether people truly believe that their old furniture has problems, they eagerly embrace an apparently unassailable reason for spending money on new stuff. Many organizations have replaced their office furniture in order to be sure of complying with the regulations. Often their old desks would not have failed an assessment of compliance (although chairs are more at risk). Main desk surfaces do not have to move up and down on an ingenious crank system. An old-fashioned, unattractive and other-wise undesirable desk may comply perfectly well with the regulations. What the regulations, and good practice, demand of desks is simply that they be large enough so that people working at a computer screen are able to position themselves and the equipment in a variety of ways and thereby achieve a comfortable working position. If this is to allow a substantial VDU screen and keyboard to be placed together, with space for resting wrists, it needs to be at least 800 mm deep for part of the desk. The possibility of adaptable height should be considered, and furniture manufacturers making desks that adjust have tried to imply that this is a legal requirement or, at least, a good way of complying with the law. It may be helpful, particularly if someone is certain to sit at the same desk for many months or years. It can often be achieved with panel-hung system furniture, and for keyboard-entry staff many ingenious especially adaptable solutions are also available.

Chairs and VDUs

Desk-height adjustability is less relevant than adjusting the height of a chair, a simpler, cheaper expedient. Concert pianists have long been aware of the need to place their hands at exactly the right height in relation to the keyboard. No one has ever suggested that the adjustable piano stool is a silly solution, that a better one would be to ratchet the piano keyboard up and down. A chair that can be positioned at a comfortable height is what a desk worker needs, particularly when working at an office keyboard. A foot rest must be available to allow a chair to be raised high enough for someone tall without leaving short legs dangling. For someone who is exceptionally tall it is likely that the height of a desk will need to be adjusted. In these very rare cases people are best served by having either a special desk or a standard one that has been raised up on additional supports that can move whenever the place of work is changed. A chair with a seat height that ranges from 318 mm to 410 mm will suit the majority of people, but this is a wide range, and not all products meet it. When a manufacturer offers a range of adjustability, be sure that the range described here is met, as some start well below and may not reach the upper measure. Adjustable chairs have to be strong enough to carry most people. Additional strength may be required for people who are at the extreme end of the weight scale and also for chairs used for twenty-four hours a day by shift workers, as these are subject to extra stress.

In addition to height adjustability, a chair has to satisfy other criteria. It should offer support in the lumbar region of the back, and the regulations say that the seat and back must both adjust in height. They specifically do *not* require that they should adjust separately. A fixed relation of seat and back, such as a 'shell', can comply with regulations if the whole can be raised and lowered, despite the fact that it does not provide good back support for people outside the range of the proportions for which the particular shell was devised. So in the end these regulations, having been interminably discussed by experts before being set down, have not managed to guarantee that vital necessity – lumbar support. Chairs are required to have stable bases and castors; a five-point star base is the generally recommended solution. Of the chairs intended for desk work at that exhibition mentioned at the beginning of the chapter, 95 per cent had that type of base. The features that a good chair should have are sometimes not found in the older furniture that lurks in offices. The replacement of inadequate chairs must be taken in hand. It is unlikely that new chairs bought for office use will not comply with the law, although it is wise to check. The law requires that old ones that do not comply be replaced by January 1996, but only for staff working most of the time with VDUs. This does not mean all the chairs in an organization have to be replaced. If people do not work more than a few hours a week on a VDU, then they do not have to be provided with a chair designed to meet the needs of a VDU worker. But if they do, even when they are fond of their familiar, sub-standard seating, the organization is obliged to provide one that meets the rules. Forcing someone to sit at it is

Attribute	Recommendation
Angle between seat and back	90–100°
Seat width	400 mm minimum
Seat depth	360–400 mm
Seat height	MUST be adjustable: 380–535 mm
Back height	200–500 mm
Lumbar support height	170–300
Seat height to underside of desk	minimum 70 mm
Seat height to top side of desk	210–300
Seat tilt	+ / − 5° from horizontal
Armrests	optional
Arm set back from seat front	minimum 100 mm
Arm height from seat	200–250
Arm length	minimum 200 mm
Seat, armrests, backrest	well padded
Chair covers	non-slip, easy to clean, breathable

Figure 5.2   Guidance on office chair ergonomics
Source: Adapted from HSE, *Seating at work*, London, HMSO, 1991

another matter. The arms, if there are any, should give support, for which their height may need to be adjustable. They should not catch on clothes or on the desk. The chair back can provide better lumbar support if it follows the body movement as you lean forward. Despite much research and reams of guidance, chairs do not make everyone comfortable. There is a steady market of special chairs and shops devoted entirely to supplying seating solutions for the suffering masses with back pain.

Back and other musculo-skeletal problems are a cause of many lost days of work, not to mention a considerable amount of pain. There are many good reasons, apart from the law, why suitable chairs should be provided for all desk-based staff. Simply complying with the law is not really what it is all about: there are plenty of serious physical problems associated with desk work. Many of these are the result not of bad furniture being provided but of people being unable, or unwilling, to adjust the good furniture that they have been given so that it suits their needs. If the adjustments are poorly designed, the controls are hard to find and hard to use and the instructions difficult to understand, they will not be used, and the law will have failed in its intention. Try asking the next lucky company that gets your order for 250 chairs to supply a computer disk, compatible with the software and hardware used in your organization, that can run as a screen saver on VDUs in your office and provide full pictorial and verbal instructions about how to adjust the chair and who to telephone if the adjustment does not work. Competition in the furniture industry is so acute that you may succeed in getting this written for you if it is a condition of your buying the chairs. Good luck.

How many different types of chair are needed in one organization? Like many other things, variety in chairs is used to denote status as much as different work requirements, and excessive variety reduces flexibility. Few organizations benefit from devoting management time to marshalling the right chair behind the right desk when the chairs wander or the staff numbers change. A visitor chair is required that need not be as complicated as a desk chair, since it is only for short-term use. A simple, cheap construction is more than adequate. A standard visitor chair can be used in meeting rooms or lounges and at any tables intended for meetings. The desk chair, on the castor base, can be the same for all desk-based staff. There is no need for a high back, or a different construction, or more adjustability, or a leather finish for senior staff. A chair that can be provided either with or without arms, simply by screwing on or taking off removable ones, can be the way to give the necessary variety to one chair. Variety in colour scheme is a good way of introducing colour into the office, but beware if allocating certain colours to certain areas will take up management time and effort.

The law is having an effect on available furniture products. The most important item to be affected by the regulations in this field is, as it should be, the VDU itself. Adjustability needed to reduce the strain of working at this equipment really does need to be provided. This means that some existing equipment does not comply and will have to be replaced. The position of the screen must be adjustable on a swivel or tip-tilt base; the relation of the keyboard and the screen must not be fixed; the height of the keyboard must be adjustable. Since equipment changes fast, much of it will be obsolete for other reasons before the health and safety regulations can bite, and, as we have said, new equipment is generally designed to comply with the laws. Some things need to be watched. Companies giving all their staff laptop portables need to consider the desktop availability of an independent screen. The laptop does not allow the screen and keyboard to change position in relation to each other, except by altering the angle that the screen makes with the keyboard, which is not sufficient. What that implies for people who work to a large extent from home and who use a portable laptop is not yet clear.

Cost

> 'Furniture is generally over-designed for cable management. Go for simple solutions and expect the furniture to be in use for fifteen years.'
>
> IBM's design manager in *Architects' Journal*, October 1993

You can pay anything you like for one person's furniture, from £100 for the lowliest clerk to £10,000 for the chief executive. As a general rule, you get what you pay for. The issue is: what should you pay? What is worth paying in your situation? The typical workstation, a desk, chair and local storage, has a price tag reflecting the size, the quality of construction, the details of the surface finishes, the degree of adjustability, the volume purchased, the length of guarantee, the professionalism of after-sales service – and some hard bargaining. The market is highly competitive; there are always bargains to be struck, and the list price is NEVER the real one, so discounts quoted must usually be substantial to be attractive. A basic workstation can be purchased for £500; a medium-quality one costs about £1,500. At prices below £500 you should not expect a long life or any after-sales service, and you may need to assemble some of the furniture yourself. Nor should you expect the sales representatives to understand what a British Standard is, let alone know if their product complies. Prices over £1,500 cover higher quality, more expensive finishes and unusual designs. An office chair with all necessary adjustability to meet health and safety requirements, purchased from suppliers of office stationery and equipment, may cost as little as £25, but £150 buys a far more robust and attractive product. At the high design end are chairs costing over £500. The bulk of the furniture budget goes to individual workstations, but do not forget the cost of furniture in meeting rooms and reception and amenity areas, which could add 25 per cent or more to the final furniture bill.

A beauty parade

> *'You can have any colour you want – as long as it's black.'*
> Attributed to Henry Ford as a selling point for the Model T Ford

Choices have to be made. Should they be democratic? Should the cost decide comfort levels? When an investment is made in new furniture, it makes simple sense to ensure that the majority of the people who will use it find it acceptable. This need not mean letting everyone have a say – representatives can play an active role on behalf of the majority – nor does it mean that views expressed through representatives can all necessarily be acted on, even though they may be listened to. Cost must obviously be an important factor. Within any cost range, suited to the budget available, there are always a number of choices. Once the shortlist has been chosen, a beauty parade has much to commend it in helping you to reach the final decision.

Ask the selected shortlist of suppliers to provide a mock-up of a workstation. Mock-ups can be brought in to let people see them or even be placed on the office floor and actually used by various members of staff. The mock-ups must be of a typical workstation. Each supplier should provide an identical arrangement as far as their product range allows: a desk of the same size and shape, with the same amount of under-desk storage, and the same types of local free-standing or screen-mounted storage. A chair is needed too. If different suppliers are used for desks, storage and chairs, record-keeping about who has supplied what needs to be meticulous, and possible choices need to be clarified. Chair A can be placed with desk B and cupboard C if they are all from independent suppliers.

The choice of performance requirements should have restricted your inquiries so that only firms making things that you want are inspected. The beauty parade establishes whether the workstation works the way you and the users want it to and have assumed that it does, whether one works better than another or fits your image better. The choice now comes down to things that matter. Does the edge of the desk snag your stockings when you get up? Is the colour, sheen and feel of the finish acceptable? Are the legs supporting the desk in the way of your own when you sit down? Can you put the cables in and out of the cable tray when you want to change the computer on your desk? (Whether or not there is a cable tray should have been dealt with by the specification for each mock-up in the first place.) Is it easy to slide the chair under the desk? When you get up, do the arms wedge under the desktop? Is the pen tray in the pedestal functional? Can you fit your files into the storage units? Does the desk drawer open fully and smoothly?

Careful labelling of the items being judged is essential. Do not depend on a description of their virtues by the salesmen vying with each other for business. A simple questionnaire, allowing space for a clear statement of preferences and judgements, needs to be filled in by all who inspect the workstations. Labels on the items may usefully give the cost of each. People need to be credited with enough intelligence to judge value for money. A marginally more alluring finish is unlikely to be credited with sufficient benefit to justify a doubling of the price. An irritating pen tray may not rule out the desk that is demonstrably better value for money. When users appreciate the real costs they are less likely to behave childishly about minor problems. Any special features need to be examined by those who are most affected. In an organization where everyone uses VDUs and cable management is vital, the opinion of the IT department must be sought. If there are complex filing requirements the relevant group needs to be involved. If footrests are being ordered for some people, ensure that they are tried out in advance by those who will use them. Having displayed the workstations and received the ratings of the user representatives, the choice remains that of the management. Representatives should not expect that what they say they like will automatically be what they get – public relations and communications have to be better than that for a successful participatory choice. Managers need to be aware of the feelings of the body of people likely to use the workstations and to know that if they choose the least popular one, there had better be good reasons.

Let there be light

> *'I was to share a small, untidy office with Noreen. It was defined by modern partitions, but there were ragged holes in them that looked as though they had been chewed away by the cables that flopped out of them. Ducting and cables dangled from the ceiling. It was hot and airless. It smelt of stale tobacco and wet plaster. There was no natural light. We were illuminated by a fluorescent tube and a wooden standard-lamp that was the personal property of Noreen's auntie.'*
>
> J. Mole, *Brits at Work*, p. 86

How much light should you have? Does everyone need a desk lamp of their own? There are shifting standards in the amount of light that should be provided, which are considered in chapter 6. What must also be noted is that if an engineer is asked to specify a lighting system to produce a particular light level, you may well get one that provides a much higher level when the lamp bulbs are new. The engineer has automatically taken account of the fact that the light output of a lamp diminishes as it gets older. If the diffuser on the fitting never gets cleaned, this compounds the light loss. It is not necessary to provide each person with their own desk lamp – task light, as they are called. A well-designed lighting system can deliver suitable light to each desk, as well as different light levels in areas that need them. Not all lighting systems are well designed, so if a separate light is specifically needed, it can still be provided, bearing in mind that it needs its own power outlet and should be securely fixed so that it cannot be dislodged from its position as people brush past.

Many new office buildings are equipped with a basic lighting system that the new occupier instantly wishes to replace or supplement, from Noreen's auntie or any other source, as it does not provide the amount and type of light that is required. This is, of course, not the case only in new office buildings. Old ones too may suffer from inappropriate lighting. In a new building it seems less excusable, as the right decisions for today's needs to be well served by today's technology could surely have been taken at the outset. Common sense tells you that you are looking for light that will not give people headaches, that will not get left on when not needed, that will not reflect off computer screens so that the only thing to be seen on the screen is the pattern of lights on the ceiling. The problem comes with a range of issues and choices to be navigated; halogen, tungsten, metal halide, UV radiation, uplighters, energy efficiency, movement-sensor control, daylight-corrected fluorescent fittings ... Is another specialist needed to sort through all these new-fangled ideas? There is a danger that the specialist may be so taken with the special properties of the many available lights that the building manager will end up having to stock fifty-seven varieties of light bulbs, each matched to different situations in the building: the general office floors, the atrium spotlights six storeys up in the air, the dining area and the lit-up self-service chilled-food cabinets, the front hall, the chairman's desk lamp, the reading area in the library, not to mention the conference room and its projectors. The lighting specifier should be asked to keep track of the types of fitting, check the bulb types and, once their number reaches about ten, try to find fittings that use the same bulbs as fittings already chosen. (The office with the 1,000 dud pedestals described earlier also has a janitor's store that has to carry an inventory of thirty-five types of light bulbs. Long-term management of this building had been ignored in more than one area.)

It should not be an opaque problem. People generally like the tungsten – incandescent – lights to which they are accustomed at home, but these are not very bright, give off a lot of heat and are unsuitable for large areas of general lighting, such as offices. Fluorescent lights suffer from flicker, poor colour values that make the environment look a sickly yellow and badly designed fittings that are unattractive and hard to clean. The many old-fashioned installations still around are enough to give fluorescent lights a bad name with many office workers. This is to some extent unjustified. Today there are many fittings and types of tube that provide glare-free light of a suitable colour and give a good quality of light. To replace the fittings in an existing installation may be trickier than creating a new installation, as the existing ceiling has to be suited to the new fittings unless the whole ceiling is replaced.

Brighter halogen lights have been developed in the search for better ways to light large spaces. These give out good, bright light, but they have other problems. The fittings get too hot to touch safely and must not be placed near combustible materials; they require transformers to modify the power input; the light is too bright to look at directly without getting after-images; and, if unprotected by glass, they give out an unacceptably high level of ultraviolet radiation. Despite all these drawbacks, when halogen lights are used as uplighters they give an attractive general light that is also suitable for office workers seated at VDU screens. Their main benefit is that their light is diffuse, because it is reflected rather than direct, so that there is little likelihood of distracting reflections. A space lit by uplighters must not be too low and must have flat white or very light-coloured surfaces off which the light can be reflected. A ceiling height of at least 3 to 3.5 metres is best. The fitting will fry the ceiling if it is closer than about 0.8 metres, and when the light is bounced off the reflecting surface it must be able to spread over a considerable distance, otherwise too many fittings would be needed. The fittings must be well above eye-level. Metal halide lights are also used as uplighters. The main disadvantage of these is that they take some time to warm up. They may be switched on at the beginning of the day and left on all day, but as they take about ten minutes to reach their full intensity they are quite unsuitable for places where the light can be turned off several times in the course of the day either because the available daylight is strong enough without added artificial light or because there is no one in the space, so that for energy-saving reasons the light should be turned off.

Save energy: turn it off

Stickers by the light switch never saved much money. People are fallible and forget to act on them, especially in large, shared areas where no one feels responsible for the general environment. So automated systems have been developed. There are many complex electronic and mechanical systems for controlling the amount of time that lights are on in offices. They depend on a variety of technologies. Photoelectric cells determine whether there is insufficient natural daylight and, if so, switch on the artificial lights. Movement sensors turn *on* lights if they detect movement. If the occupant of the room is asleep, or hiding under the desk, the lights go out. If he is stock-still, thinking profoundly, he will have to flap his arms like a scarecrow from time to time to keep the light on. Other systems operate on a simple time-switch basis. Any light that has been switched on will be switched off at, say, lunchtime, at the end of the average working day and at chosen times, such as half an hour after the cleaners should have gone home. If people are working in the space at the time or come in subsequently and need light, they must switch it on. This system deals with forgetfulness or flagrant carelessness and lights left on potentially forever once they have been switched on but does not attempt to use sophisticated technology to decide if the light is needed at all. It can be irritating to have a light switched off while you are working, and it is more than irritating if light switches are far away, hard to reach or badly labelled so it is unclear which you need to use.

In the USA, because of the energy-saving fittings that have been introduced into modern offices, several utility companies have been able to avoid building expensive new power stations, and they actively promote the use of such lighting. This indicates the enormous amount of energy used by office lighting. To reduce the heat output of the lights by means of energy-efficient fittings is frequently the most effective way of saving energy. The energy used by the lights themselves is reduced, as is any energy needed for cooling to compensate for the heat generated by the lights. The extent of such saving varies in different climates and building orientations, but even in the temperate climate of the UK the heat given off by lights and electronic equipment together can make it hard to create a comfortable working environment on a hot summer's day (see chapter 8).

Where is the switch? How many lights does it control? And who gets to use it? These are vital questions in determining the way lights are used, how much energy they mop up and how satisified people are with their working environment. Individual control is much prized by staff. Those without control feel that their working environment has become hostile and inhuman. The pull switch dangling overhead may look ridiculous, and it is certainly a problem if the only way to switch off rows of fittings when people have gone home is to stroll down the aisles pulling each switch. But it gives people a sense of control over their immediate needs. In the next chapter research is discussed that considers how far the ability to change and retain some control of one's workplace is crucial to satisfaction.

Summary

This chapter helps you pick a way through a maze of decisions to be made when choosing furniture and lighting and offers a process whereby this can readily be done.

Furniture is used to convey status and image as well as having function. There is so much to choose from on the market that it can be difficult to distinguish priorities. There are two different types of furniture: systems, where all the parts are interdependent, or separate items that can be combined in many different groupings. Systems are more constraining and more orderly. Mix and match can allow for specific needs to be met by all the different elements.

Storage is one of the most crucial elements in office furniture. Units that allow lateral filing can accommodate more material on a smaller 'footprint' than traditional filing cabinets, especially if additional height is also possible. Specialist storage furniture companies have developed elaborate ranges. The image of wood versus that of metal has to be considered in the light of the robustness and neatness of design that metal can provide. Expensive, high-density storage units can be extremely useful. However, the costs are high; the limits are not fully understood; and they can introduce inflexibility. The requirement of a 'mobile' worker, who is not always based in the same place, has only just begun to be considered. New furniture types are coming on to the market that will prove very useful for these workers.

The new health and safety guidelines and EC regulations are being exploited by manufacturers who make it sound as if the old furniture you have breaks the law. The furniture, as opposed to VDU equipment, has only a few conditions with which it must comply: the desk must be large enough to accommodate a VDU in a variety of positions; a depth of 800 mm is generally ample. A footrest must be available if requested. The chair must have a seat and back that can be raised and lowered. The back does not need to be independently adjustable.

The cost range for furniture is enormous, just as the variety available is mind-boggling. There can be a thirtyfold difference in the cost of a chair. If you are planning to spend £2,000 to £5,000 per workstation it is vital to get the choice right. A beauty parade at which possible products are reviewed and judged is a good mechanism for involving staff in a decision that affects them all. The choice cannot be wholly democratic at these sorts of prices, but some items fall easily within the remit of a user group. The colour of chair fabric, for example, is something that can be chosen by staff representatives.

Lighting has many possible solutions. The much maligned fluorescent tube has been greatly improved and can provide a satisfactory solution. Other aproaches, in particular uplighting, have benefits. Energy-saving devices need to be considerd early on in the building design. A control system can be incorporated as an element of the lighting installation. Relying on individuals to switch off lights is unlikely to make savings, but, if possible, people should be allowed the freedom to switch lights on and off for themselves if they feel the need.

6 'SBS' and All That

When the clerk suggested that the pernicious symptoms of 'sick building syndrome' might be moderated through the introduction of a shovelful of coal to the fire, Mr Scrooge replied, 'Bah, humbug!'

> 'The maladies that afflict clerks ... arise from three causes: first, constant sitting, secondly the incessant movement of the hand and always in the same direction, thirdly, the strain on the mind ... what tortures these workers most acutely is the intense and incessant application of the mind, for in such work as this, the whole brain, its nerves and fibres, must be kept constantly on the stretch; hence ensues loss of <u>tonus.</u> From this result headaches, heavy colds, sore throats and fluxes to the eyes from keeping them fixed on the paper.'
>
> Bernardino Ramazzini, 'Diseases of Workers', translated from the Latin text *De morbis artificium*, 1713

So do buildings make you sick?

Is it the building, or your job, or the boss? Every day new health hazards devised by mankind are identified. Coal mining, forestry and construction work all seem intrinsically dangerous. By contrast, it seems incongruous to associate ill health with sedentary office work – so blame the building. The maladies described by Ramazzini, and assumed to be an occupational hazard, are still suffered by 'clerks'. More than 250 years after Ramazzini's description an apparently new scourge has emerged, 'sick building syndrome' or SBS for short. This, by the way, is not the same problem as 'building-related illness'. Some illnesses are contracted by people as a direct result of some aspect of a particular building, though not necessarily a building where they work. Micro-organisms, indisputably identifiable and causing some very nasty illnesses, are sometimes found in, say, the water supply in a building. Legionnaires' disease, for example, has killed a number of unfortunate people, and buildings are clearly implicated. Serious illness, such as humidifier fever and legionnaires' disease, must be guarded against. Ways in which these can be transmitted and prevented are clearly understood, and suitable measures to determine whether your building is at risk and, if so, taking appropriate action need not cost an arm and a leg. For example, regular monthly testing for the presence of legionella bacteria in cooling systems for air conditioning has become standard practice for efficient building managers, against whom a charge of negligence might be levelled if they failed to organize the tests. In other cases, though health consequences are taken seriously, the action taken is not necessarily effective. Asbestos has been clearly linked to asbestosis, an unpleasant and debilitating lung disease, and a specific type of asbestos to a fatal form of cancer. Millions of pounds' worth of work has been done to eliminate it from buildings, often creating considerable disruption, despite the fact that most asbestosis is linked not to working in a building in which asbestos was incorporated but rather with working on the processes of making or installing the material. Smoking, even passive smoking, is known to damage health (see chapter 7), yet employers are not under a specific legal obligation to ensure that their workforce is not exposed to passive smoking, though this would be relatively cheap to achieve.

Less fatal and much more difficult to pin down is 'sick building syndrome'. It describes a group of ailments, including headaches, dry throat, sore eyes, lethargy, blocked and stuffy nose, and dry or itchy skin. These symptoms, as a cluster, have come to be causally associated with buildings, especially offices, though it is worth observing that a few of them are also associated with winter coughs and colds. When a significant number of occupants suffer from this group of symptoms, and when they say that their symptoms diminish or disappear when they are not in the office, researchers have drawn the conclusion that it is the office building that is causing the problem. This has been eagerly pounced on as an idea by the media, who like a good disaster, and by people marketing services designed to detect and clear up the problem. 'SBS' is said to lead to days off work, so the company suffers loss, staff suffer discomfort and are demotivated and the cause of the problem cannot be easily identified and cured. Are there really symptoms that people get just because of the building they work in? Should you worry about all this?

> *'If they get a bit of a headache, feel a bit sick, their eyes itch, then it is much more difficult to trace the cause. There are about 28,000 things in the built environment that can cause people's eyes to itch. Even then, with a bit of luck you can sort it out. But it's difficult, expensive and can take a long time. You need a team of about twenty people, and you can spend a third of a million pounds looking at a big building.'*
>
> Professor Patrick O'Sullivan, interviewed for *UCL Universe*, 1993

What is the chance that your building hosts one or more of those 28,000 itch-inducing substances? With that many possible causes, it seems highly likely. But it will probably be difficult to identify which are actually present and in unacceptable – but measurable – quantities. It may be even harder to link the presence of the substances with the symptoms reported by the staff. Then eliminating them or preventing them from affecting the staff may be impossible. No wonder it may cost a third of a million pounds. Sampling and testing for a known problem in a known location, as is required when controlling legionnaires' disease, is a manageable proposition. Tracking down unknown agents for an unspecific problem can be frighteningly expensive because the number of possible items to test for is large, the quantities of the offending agents may be small, so that detection equipment and tests are complex and costly, and the ways in which they affect people may differ. This is amply demonstrated by allergies. Some individuals can be nearly incapacitated by a substance that others are never aware they are inhaling, ingesting or touching. Identifying unusual allergenic agents can take a great many tests. These are real difficulties. But if the tests do not produce results, spending the money may not be worth while. And will failure be even more expensive? Litigation against companies by their employees is increasingly frequent, particularly in the USA. Successful litigation on account of 'SBS' has not yet been achieved, though it has been attempted. Perhaps the problems associated with 'SBS' will join the list of reasons why employers are taken to court. Then you will really have to worry if the connection between building and 'sickness' can be proved incontrovertibly.

It has come to be accepted, as a result of research projects carried out in a number of different countries, that the syndrome is real – that something about buildings is able to make people unwell, not merely feel uncomfortable. As yet, however, research has not pinned down what it is about buildings that causes the 'sickness'. Various culprits have been named. Air-conditioning, noxious gases, negative ions and dust mites have all been implicated. There is a consensus of a kind, particularly among office workers in the UK, that air-conditioning has bad effects on people. An air-conditioned building must be sealed from penetration by outside air and this has led to 'SBS' being described as 'tight building syndrome' in some research accounts. Another group of suspects are volatile gases, such as formaldehyde, which can be found in large quantities in new buildings, as they are used in the manufacture of such things as carpets, furniture and wall materials. Volatile gases sometimes smell nasty, and it is possible that some people are actually allergic to them. Or take dust mites. They inhabit fabric, live off flakes of dead skin and multiply happily on the warm seat of your office chair. They do not bite, but some people may be badly affected by these microscopic creatures and their by-products. These are only some of the front runners under consideration in the search for a solution to 'SBS'. All the agents that could be associated, individually or in combination, with the reported symptoms have not been clearly identified. Another approach is also receiving increasing attention. It is suggested that when people perceive that they can control their working environment by changing, say, temperature, air movement or lighting, they avoid the symptoms of illness suffered by those whose perception is that their environment is beyond their personal control.

> *'I have experienced sore throats/colds recently. Must be associated with the move of office.'*
>
> Questionnaire response from staff member after an unpopular office move

There is evidence, as we have said, that people who work in office buildings suffer from a range of symptoms embraced by the various descriptions of 'SBS'. What is hard to establish is whether the level experienced in some buildings is above the normal level to be expected in a randomly selected group. Do these symptoms occur anyway, because of people's general health, or are they related to factors such as the type of work people do or their psycho-social situation – the boss or the spouse? If buildings are to blame, is it the office or the home? Could the culprit even be the journey in between? Some sufferers say that the symptoms improve or disappear when they leave the office building. As a sceptical manager, you may wish not to put too much trust in this claim or in answers to the question of whether people have suffered from a particular symptom 'in the last year'. Recall is not infallible over this length of time – a few weeks is the most that people can remember accurately. Much of the research into 'SBS' is marred by unreliable information gleaned from questionnaires and so far has not demonstrated incontrovertibly that any syndrome linking the symptoms firmly to office buildings really does exist.

None the less, 'sick buildings' are newsworthy; occupants are persuaded of the truth of the proposition that some office buildings make you 'sick'. If a building is suspected of being 'sick', it attracts attention.

A multi-storey office tower in the Midlands was featured in a television programme on sick building syndrome. Staff complained eloquently of their difficult working conditions – they were tired, had headaches, sore eyes and runny noses, experienced difficulty in concentration and felt generally miserable. Absenteeism was high. The building was blamed for their problems. Following transmission of the documentary, studies were commissioned to identify and solve the problems. Specialists crawled over every inch of the building. They could find few problems. The main failing seemed to be poor management of the air-conditioning system – it was not operated according to its design, hence some areas were far too hot, others too cold. A new firm was brought in to operate the air-conditioning, and their work was closely monitored. Complaints from staff working in the building fell dramatically. To the occupants the building was no longer 'sick'.

A couple of years later the building changed hands. Staff in another organization were informed that they would soon be moving into that building. They remembered the TV programme and were sure that it was a 'sick building'. They generated enormous resistance to the move. Moving there was seen as proof that management did not care about their employees or their working conditions. Unions contributed to the outcry. More studies were commissioned. More specialists crawled over the building. They found very little that was untoward. Staff resistance continued – the label 'stick building' clung on tenaciously. Eventually, management and staff agreed to the move, but that the building would be totally redesigned before they did so. All windows would be replaced, all the air-conditioning would be

> changed, as would most of the plant that controlled it. The bill was tens of millions of pounds, and there were a couple of years of delay during negotiations and building work, just to remove the damaging 'sick building' label.

Such an episode, of course, does not prove that no buildings are ever 'sick'. It does suggest that the second set of remedial actions and costs may have provided little measurable benefit. If it is not proven that 'SBS' is a measurable phenomenon against which action can be taken, what other approaches are there to achieving a healthy, happy workforce?

Comfort

The charter of the National Union of Clerks at the beginning of this century was not only concerned with wages and hours but also demanded 'Healthy *and comfortable* offices where they [clerks] can work and keep a sound mind in a healthy body'.

Take a step sideways for a moment. Without needing to be committed over the issue of whether your building makes you or your staff sick, consider whether a building can contribute to comfort – or, rather, to discomfort. The general consensus is 'yes'. Most people can identify situations when they are uncomfortable for which they blame the building. A definition of comfort is not easy to come by, as it varies for different people. Men and women, for example, do not find the same conditions comfortable. This need not surprise anyone. For a start, the clothes that they wear are usually of quite different weight. Physiology also affects comfort. None the less, comfort may be a more manageable topic than 'SBS', as it is more familiar territory, it deals with fewer possible variables and most reasonable people are already aware that it is not an absolute measure.

Comfort is generally considered to be related to temperature, relative humidity, air movement and probably light and noise levels. Generally acceptable standards have been proposed in a variety of guidelines and regulations for building design, but consensus has not been reached. Some years ago designers were told to provide lighting levels of 1,000 lux for office work, then 500 lux, and now 350 is thought to be enough except for some visually highly demanding jobs, such as working at a drawing board. For those working on computer screens the parameters have changed again, as glare and the veiling of reflections are as much of concern as absolute lux levels. Comfortable temperature levels are no more firmly established. Ignoring for a moment the technical difference between 'radiant' and 'dry-bulb' temperature measures, the range for comfort in sedentary work recommended by the UK Health and Safety Executive, whose mission is the health of people in the workplace, is 21–24° Centigrade (70–75° Fahrenheit) ambient air temperature. An allowance of plus or minus one (or two) degrees is sometimes included in a statement of a target range. The blurring of the edges of the range need not be taken to indicate sloppiness. After all, the concept is not precise: temperature changes through the day; measuring instruments may be only approximately calibrated or inefficiently used; and people differ about what they consider comfortable. What is a little confusing, however, is the UK government regulation that buildings that are occupied by civil servants should not be heated to temperatures above 19° Centrigrade (66° Fahrenheit). This is part of a laudable effort to conserve energy but somewhat misses the comfort target if the range of 21–24 degrees is accepted. Even if the extra plus or minus one or two degrees is allowed for, 19 degrees barely makes it into the bottom of the range. Common sense tells you that a howling draft or freezing ankles and a hot head are rarely popular. An acceptable differential of three degrees between the temperature at ankle height and that at head height, and a maximum air speed of 1.5 metres per second, are also part of recommended standards for comfort. Indeed, the definition of comfort in these standards, that 90 per cent of those exposed to the conditions should find them acceptable, may not be capable of a proof more scientific than common sense.

Does the lack of a single, accepted set of guidelines mean that it is impossible to provide a building in which most people feel comfortable? Not at all. Temperature and relative humidity together are more important for comfort than either on their own. In temperate climates such as the UK and much of Europe, North American and Australia, these are not often far outside the broad range that would enable most people to be comfortable. No excessive effort is needed to modify them. A well-built building, with windows that do not leak and a good level of insulation, served by a simple radiator-based heating system for winter months, is often perfectly adequate and should offer a comfortable environment. This being so, it is depressing how often buildings are, in fact, *not* comfortable. Often the problem is related to modification of temperature. In some buildings one side roasts in the sun, while the other is chilled. If the heating system is designed without local controls, this is hard to regulate. In others, the air feels warm and stale, but when windows are opened for ventilation, the traffic noise is deafening, papers are tossed by the wind, grit is blown into the coffee. (In some you may get a hernia just trying to open the window.) In yet others the radiators belt out heat regardless of the outside temperature in obedience to the calendar: 'If it is after 1 October, it is cold.'

> *'Overshoes and topcoats may not be worn in the office, but neck scarves and headgear may be worn in inclement weather . . . it is recommended that each member of the clerical staff shall bring four pounds of coal each day during cold weather.'*
>
> Midland firm's directives on heating, 1852

These clerks, able to throw their own fuel on the fire and get up a blaze, may have been happier than you think. Recent research indicates that when people feel that they are able to make local adjustments to temperature, ventilation and lighting to suit their own immediate needs, the range of conditions that they are willing to tolerate as 'comfortable' widens; they feel less frustrated by imperfections. If there is a window to open or close, a thermostat to turn up or down, a light switch or a blind to modify the amount and quality of light, people feel they are in control. When these are not available, the next best thing is a building manager who will listen to the problem and react fast to make the necessary adjustments. Confronted by a monolithic system, where the lights can only be switched on and off centrally regardless of which bit of the building benefits from daylight, where flickering tubes are replaced weeks after being reported, where the heating controls cannot be adjusted to take account of local needs, and where there is a maintenance man who never answers the telephone and is unfriendly when you do manage to contact him, discomfort becomes more objectionable. When you are unable to turn down the heat, the slight headache building up may feel more important, because you believe, probably rightly, that if you could adjust the temperature it would get better. Multiplying this by dozens or hundreds of experiences sets the scene for the birth of the idea of a 'sick building'.

Air-conditioning

Air-conditioning is a prime example of a system that is likely to be too complex, sensitive and monolithic to permit local control. Instead, it provides ample opportunity for frustration. The simple message here is:

do not have air-conditioning in your building if you do not have to. Whether it causes sickness or not, air-conditioning is the focus of much discontent. It is also far more expensive to provide than natural ventilation. Capital costs are 20–30 per cent higher; the landlord's service charges for an air-conditioned building may be twice as much; and annual running costs can be three times as much. And in exchange for all that extra expense you may get only more complaints. The extra running cost represents extra energy use, which makes it less environmentally responsible as well. A combination of factors makes air-conditioning unpopular. In the first place, systems frequently do not work as users expect, nor as they were designed by engineers. Long periods spent fine-tuning sometimes fail entirely to bring them up to the desired performance level. Sometimes details are badly designed. Delivered temperature levels and speed of air movement are not always acceptable and the noise of rushing air can be irritating. Smells may be transmitted from one area to another within the system, and more often than seems possible a 'fresh'-air intake is located where it sucks in smells from, say, an adjacent kitchen exhaust. Many systems recirculate some of the extracted, 'used' indoor air to reduce the cost of raising or cooling raw outside air to the desired temperature. When filters are not properly cleaned and maintained, the system can transport unwanted pollutants (germs that hover among those with coughs and colds or substances that cause allergic reactions) all over the building with maximum efficiency. Reasons for the wide range of problems experienced with air-conditioning include incorrect commissioning (starting up), so that the system never even starts working the way it was designed; too much complexity in the design, so that there are lots of bits to go wrong; poor management and maintenance, so that the system progressively deteriorates; and the destruction of the balance of air in/air out by placing partitions that had not been anticipated when the system was designed.

Developers and estate agents, influenced by multinational clients used to more extreme climates, and by aspirations for larger returns from more expensive properties, have put office users and purchasers under pressure to demand air-conditioning as essential in a 'high-quality' building. It is not. There are, of course, some situations where even in a mild climate it brings benefits. It can be used to exclude dirt and noise generated in central urban areas, especially on traffic arteries. It can make it possible to create internal rooms such as lecture theatres, which do not require windows, or to use very deep spaces where windows cannot supply sufficient ventilation to the central areas. It can keep areas filled with heat-producing equipment, such as computer rooms or reprographic facilities, at suitable temperatures for both people and the equipment itself. Where specific benefits of this type are not required, resist the temptation to believe that air-conditioning makes the office a more prestigious place and impresses clients, sponsors or staff. If possible, occupy a building that is designed not to need air-conditioning, one where natural ventilation, or at most mechanical ventilation, is used for cooling, with a simple radiator-based heating system. This is not an obvious option in, say, New York where summer temperatures and relative humidity rise to extremely uncomfortable levels. Even when summer outdoor temperatures are high, well-designed openings, which provide sun-shading and allow cross ventilation, can go a long way towards keeping people comfortable. Rarely do staff in naturally ventilated UK office buildings gasp for air on sweltering summer days. It can happen, but an office full of fans whirring is as likely to be the result of high temperatures caused by heat generated inside the building, particularly by lighting and maybe also by computing equipment, as from high outdoor temperatures.

If this is not possible, and you have to accept air-conditioning, make sure that the system is sensibly zoned – that is, designed to serve areas that have different requirements using separate controls and appropriate equipment. As an example, zoning a system so that each floor of an office building is separately controlled will be necessary if several organizations occupy each floor independently, as they may have different needs. If distinct areas on a single floor have varying needs (say, because the south face of the building gets much hotter than the north), the floors may need to be further subdivided into separate air-conditioning control zones. When a building is advertised as having a flexible system that can be adjusted to suit the needs of any tenant, check that the locations of air intakes and outlets can be placed where *you* will need them and that the overall capacity and control system will suit all the different areas *you* will occupy. Then see that the system is properly used and well maintained. Expert advice will probably be needed for this, but a short visit to the plant room may tell you a lot about quality control in that department.

Windows

Windows are a brilliant invention. They let in light, keep out heat, cold, dirt and noise, and provide a view. They are also a point of weakness through which unwanted people can get in or cause damage. The most common image of an office building today is one where on all façades, at all heights above the ground, the windows are identically designed. This makes it harder for them to do the jobs they are there for, as conditions change with the orientation of the sun, the height above a noise source, the view or the potential intruder.

Well-designed windows are needed to create comfortable conditions. Size and shape are important, but they are not all that window design is about. There are many other decisions to be made. On a south-facing façade, where heat gain in summer needs to be controlled, double glazing, special heat-reflecting glass, film, external screening, deep reveals and blinds are all useful devices. The benefits are purchased at additional capital cost, but all these devices should be considered. They also help in controlling glare. Blinds that can be used variably to shut out glare as the sun changes position are usually needed where people use VDUs. The amount of light coming in changes from the top to the bottom of a window, especially if sky shows at the top and land below, so horizontal slatted blinds, or full screening types, perform more efficiently than blinds with vertical slats in cutting down glare. For any blind the controls must be easily reached. It is sobering to discover how often controls are inaccessible – too high, behind screens, across wide pieces of furniture. This is a design failing that also frequently applies to levers and locks for opening the windows.

The carpet debate

It has become standard to carpet office buildings. Carpets bring colour and individuality to a room; weaving in new patterns and customized designs is not difficult. Carpets have replaced wooden floors or substances like linoleum, making a warmer, and – of significance in open plan – a quieter environment. Much research has been done to create fibres and weaves that suit every budget, are hard-wearing and easy to clean and resist the build-up of static electricity caused by the friction of people walking on them. The results have been reasonably successful, and suppliers, consultants and cleaning companies will give advice about the products that are succeeding best at any particular time.

Problems with computers spurred the development of anti-static fibres, but static may affect some individuals badly too. Another problem is that the off-gassing of the glues used in their construction when they are newly installed, and the release of fibres into the air as they are abraded, could contribute to the poor air qualilty that is associated with 'SBS'. There is little proof of this, though the Scandinavians are returning to wooden floors, ostensibly for this reason. Of course, they do grow a lot of trees in Scandinavia, which may be influencing this fashion. On the other side of the world the Japanese are only gradually moving to carpeted offices from linoleum or other hard finishes. The carpet debate has not yet been resolved.

Cleanliness is next to healthiness

Thorough cleaning is often the key to providing an environment that is healthy. This does not just mean having doormats that extend far enough to capture most of the outside dirt from shoes, powerful vacuum cleaners efficiently and frequently used and a contract with a specialist firm to bring sparkle to the loos. It is about cleaning the parts other cleaners do not reach, the ones that cannot be seen – the ductwork and filters for an air-conditioning or ventilation system. These are in a position to deliver dirty air as easily as clean. The first point at which cleanliness starts to matter here is installation. A clean building site reduces the chance of the wrong things getting left behind in the duct in the first place. Once installed, a maintenance schedule that acknowledges the need for cleanliness can keep air-handling systems working more efficiently. Voids under raised floors can also provide a home for dirt, and occasionally pests, if not kept clean during and after construction.

Watch out for water. Water supplies can harbour potentially harmful bacteria. Tests are easy to carry out and occasionally reveal unwanted coliforms in taps in kitchens or teapoints. Usually the bacteria found in these tests are themselves intrinsically harmless but are an indication that more harmful ones may be present. Water coolers and vending machines are more frequently found to be contaminated. They need conscientious maintenance and cleaning.

Know your environment; monitor it

Buildings do not always deliver an environment that falls within acceptable ranges. The first requirement is, as always, to know what is going on. Knowledge – of temperature patterns by time and place, whether carbon-dioxide levels are high enough to make people feel sleepy, how much light is reaching the desks, how noisy the rooms are, whether the water supply is breeding bacteria – is important management information. This type of information should be collected regularly and systematically, if there are complaints, if not routinely. Some checks can be done by anyone with very simple equipment, such as thermometers and light or sound meters. Others require more sophisticated equipment, which may need special calibration or expertise. With good information it is possible to anticipate problems rather than being forced to react to them. It may also help to ensure that comfortable conditions are achieved and maintained and thus reduce the likelihood that your building will be found to be 'sick'.

Summary

This chapter puts the problem of 'sick' buildings into perspective and helps to return the focus of attention to measures that can be taken to optimize conditions for people working in offices.

Office workers have suffered 'sickness' for centuries. Infectious diseases, such as legionnaires' disease, in the transmission of which building services and systems play a role, are in a different category and need stringent measures to guard against them. The cluster of symptoms, including headaches, lethargy, stuffed or runny nose and itchy eyes, referred to as SBS are much less easily connected to buildings. Possible causes, such as air-conditioning, dust mites and volatile gases, have been suggested. There are a very large number of possible agents for some symptoms, and identifying and dealing with them can be extremely expensive. There is no proof that specific attributes of buildings cause the symptoms in question, and seeking to eliminate the problem by getting rid of a specific cause may not be cost-effective.

Comfort is an important goal. Temperature, relative humidity, airflow rate, light and noise contribute to comfort. A building modifies these conditions, and if acceptable levels are not achieved, the building can be said to affect comfort. Generally agreed levels of comfort are difficult to establish, as standards vary. The modification of temperature is often a crucial area in which success or failure resides.

Air-conditioning is frequently implicated when people are uncomfortable. It is not essential in temperate climates and should be avoided where possible. The costs are not justified if the results are complaints. The complexity of systems, the low levels of maintenance and management, the constraints on people's ability to modify their immediate environment or, in the longer run, replan its layout, all contribute to its unpopularity.

The design of windows must ensure that they perform in all the ways that they should. They have often been treated solely as a visual feature of the elevation, with no variation in design as different conditions demand. Windows provide a wide range of ways to increase comfort: double glazing, special glass, shading internally and externally.

Carpets, taken for granted in quality offices in many countries, are a relatively new introduction. They offer a domestic feel, an opportunity for colour, noise absorption. They have disadvantages in the form of static build-up, off-gassing when new and increased fluff in the air, which may be inhaled. Some organizations in Scandinavia have deemed it better to provide hard floor finishes in offices for these reasons.

Monitoring environmental conditions and gathering accurate information, as with all issues, is essential. It can help you to create comfort and to anticipate rather than react to problems.

7 Amenities – Luxuries or Necessities?

'Workplace, sir? That's in the prefabs round the back.'

Rising staff expectations in the developed world mean that many office buildings now offer far more than a basic working environment. This is in complete contrast to other developments that are making the office building less central to the lives of some people, who spend less time there and have freedom to work wherever it suits them. Large offices and headquarters buildings have grown so complex that they have become small communities, with places to learn, to eat, to shop, to exercise, to be entertained.

A prestigious office in Helsinki is likely to have a well-appointed sauna in the building, available to staff for their leisure and used as part of the paraphernalia surrounding an elegantly conducted meeting with important clients or colleagues. In Britain new offices in Leeds, shared by several government departments, are equipped with generous sports facilities, catering and accommodation for leisure pursuits. One of the first post-war buildings to be considered for listing in England, the office of Willis Faber Dumas in Ipswich, was built with a swimming pool inside the building as well as a turfed roof garden for the leisure needs of the staff. Why? Surely people go to the office to work. You'd think the last place they wanted to spend their leisure time was at the office. If they go to the gym during office hours, can you be sure they are giving the right amount of time to their work? An orderly world has a place for everything and everything in its place, and the office is the place for work.

Amenities: lots of them? For whom?

Additions to the office building cost money to provide and maintain. Can you afford to provide them? Can you afford *not* to provide them? The range of provision varies from country to country, company to company, building to building. Space is provided for many different activities in offices in addition to the individual work areas. These were referred to in chapter 2, when mention was made of support space. Some facilities appear to be so much part of the work requirements of the organization that they are taken for granted as part of the office. Others offer support for personal needs – that may have to be met to fulfil expectations of the workforce. They are not used as part of the job but instead in private time.

Work related amenities include:
- reception areas   a 'front door' and waiting area for visitors and a 'back door' for deliveries and waste
- reprographics   centralized photocopying and printing – almost a separate business
- conference suite   many variations, from a room with a folding wall to provision for several hundred delegates, with theatre, catering, exhibition and demonstration areas
- training suites   lecture and syndicate rooms, sometimes with sophisticated audio-visual aids
- library   active archives, also daily papers, trade magazines and reference material, comfortable seating and no disturbance from telephones

The specific details of the provision of these work-based amenities need careful consideration. How many should there be? Where should they be located? How should they be equipped and furnished? How should they be managed?

Some of the more commonly found 'personal' amenities include:
- catering   cafeterias and restaurants, kitchenettes, coffee and vending areas, tea ladies and bars
- sports   facilities range from a gym, swimming pool, sauna and games rooms inside the building, with associated showers and changing, to outdoor sports fields and club huts
- social support   first-aid room, crèche, branch of bank, travel agency particularly to assist with corporate travel arrangements, staff shops, hairdressing, medical or dental clinics (especially on isolated sites)
- smoking room   a facility where staff who need to smoke can do so and may be able to work at the same time for short periods

- transport   car parking is much in demand. Some people need bus services connecting them with town centres or linking corporate buildings
- quality of environment   enhanced by works of art and plants, as well as the overall quality, colour and finish of the work areas.

The extent to which amenities are needed or provided, and on what scale, varies. In a small building for, say, fifty people or fewer, the most that can be expected is a kitchenette for making tea and coffee. In a large office building with, say, 2,000 people, many amenities are often provided. On a large office campus in an out-of-town location most facilities are found. A sauna may never become standard in the UK; a crèche may attract little custom in the heart of a big city, a long way from home; but a canteen on a suburban industrial estate may make the difference between attracting and keeping staff or not attracting them at all.

A perk or a tool of the trade?

Part of what an office building is there for is the transactions that take place between people – the agreements, the promises, the decisions, the information exchanges. The most important transactions are not necessarily conducted in formal meetings. It has been recognized in the design of other building types that useful exchanges between people may take place, for example, in circulation routes. The corridors of power are a reality. Lobbying does take place in lobbies, as well as elsewhere. In medical surgeries patients are often less inhibited in saying what is really troubling them when they are following the doctor down the corridor than when sitting face to face in the consulting room. Important exchanges between members of the legal profession take place in the corridors around the courts in a justice building. Even if a corridor is non-committal and informal, how much nicer to conduct business in a leisure/health type of environment. In Helsinki the world of work is sufficiently civilized for it to be appropriate to conduct business in a sauna. Golf-club memberships are often given to executives in the knowledge that the club offers suitable entertainment possibilities for business colleagues that can help to lubricate business deals, with the added bonus that playing golf is a better way to keep fit, healthy and useful than performing a similar service for the company while sitting drinking in a bar. Boxes at the opera, tickets to Wimbledon, seats in the local theatre are all ways of offering business hospitality, and with the hospitality, it is assumed, some business will be transacted or at least eased, and a civilized image will be projected. This approach has long existed in the business environment. Providing decent facilities for customers in the office building is an obvious extension.

Is this sensible? What are the costs and the benefits? After all, the Willis Faber Dumas building in Ipswich, referred to earlier, is about to cover over the swimming pool in order to make more space for the expansion of staff that has inexorably taken place over the last thirty years.

Attracting and keeping staff

Amenities may be offered as a way of attracting and retaining staff. If there is nowhere to buy a meal in the vicinity, a cafeteria may be needed or at least a good kitchen in which people can prepare their own midday meal. A subsidized cafeteria may be provided, even if there are other local options, as a way of offering staff a special benefit for working with the organization. Child-care facilities fall into a similar category, being offered as a way of retaining expensively trained staff when they have young children. Another reason behind the provision of amenities may be to compensate for other losses. Staff who have recently been placed in open-plan offices or, more radical still, moved from allocated to pooled desks may be offered a staff gymnasium or games room. A decentralization policy that involves many staff in moving homes and following the employer to a new city, where people will take time to become integrated into the local scene, may be eased by providing leisure facilities on office premises that all the family can use. A large office in a remote location, or perhaps in a hostile neighbourhood, may provide some of the shops and services that are often visited in lunch hours, thus making the location more acceptable. The cost to the organization of these amenities may merely be the opportunity cost of not being able to use the space for other purposes. A commercial enterprise operating the amenity will pay rent and all its own management costs. Alternatively, the host organization may choose to incur some higher costs because it subsidizes the use of the available service – say, hairdressing or a crèche – as a way of increasing the rewards offered to staff.

The provision of office-based amenities, rather than higher pay or a shorter working week, may be beneficial to the organization. Take catering as an example. This can be very expensive – as much as £700 per person per year in all. But it need not be. Providing a subsidized canteen can cost less than a general pay rise and is easier to reverse later. A pay cut is more damaging to morale than agreeing that the canteen is losing money because no one uses it (it can be done away with) or because the prices are too low (they can be inched up). It may even be possible to dissociate the organization from the problems, as it is the catering organization that must rectify them. Intangible benefits are also assumed to flow from this type of in-house provision. Staff may take a shorter break if lunch is available on the premises. It is possible to help form a healthy workforce, or at least support those trying to eat a balanced diet, by providing a range of healthy foods. As a last resort, the space given to the cafeteria may be reclaimed if more space is urgently required for office uses, adding a little flexibility to the building.

What about a gym or sports facility? The cost of a 30-square-metre gym, suitable for a few people to work out in the lunch hour or before or after work, may not be high. It could serve perhaps 150 people. Not everyone would wish to use it, but they would all get the feeling that the management took them seriously and believed that they were worth spending money on.

Management burdens

Providing amenities requires both space and management. The host organization incurs responsibilities when it provides amenities. Every country has laws and guidelines relating to the safe design and use of specialized facilities. Even if a canteen is not aiming to promote healthy eating habits, it must not spread salmonella. A gym has to be managed so that people are aware of safe ways to use the equipment, appropriate action can be taken if there are accidents, the equipment is suitably checked for safety and stability and people are properly instructed in its use to avoid injury. Child-care facilities have to comply with a number of stringent requirements.

Is it worth the hassle for an organization whose business is not pre-school child care, or catering, or fitness and leisure management to embark on the minefield that amenities can create? Complying with the health and safety requirements associated with office work can seem onerous enough. Can you avoid making a rod for your own back?

Outsourcing will reduce the burden

To DIY or not to DIY, that is the question. The answer has changed over the last decades. In fact, the meaning of the question has changed. It used to be a question about whether to provide a particular amenity or not. It is now more likely to be about whether the amenity that staff have come to expect should be run and managed by the organization itself or 'outsourced' (another unpleasant bit of jargon) – run by an outside specialist or even by a person, team or company whose sole role is to provide essential building services for other companies, a facilities management specialist.

Back to catering as an example. It is less common for companies to hire their own kitchen staff, and manage them directly, than it was ten years ago. Tea ladies have been made redundant to be replaced by vending machines. Specialists run the kitchens and restaurants; outside suppliers have the responsibility of checking, filling and servicing the vending machines. But there can be disadvantages as well as advantages to outsourcing, whether in providing bijou executive dining, a mass-production, subsidized self-service cafeteria or phalanxes of leased coffee-making machines. In the first place, there must be a contract with the outside company. This has to be written, or at least read and managed, by someone inside the firm to be sure that it really does serve the organization's interests. To allow the caterers to write their own rules and check themselves to see that they keep them, as well as set the price for their services, would not be consistent with good management practice – obviously. As the catering firm becomes well established, serving the company from year to year, it is increasingly difficult for someone within the office organization to be fully aware of what the service could and should be like. The further away a manager is from knowing what the business – catering – is about, the harder it is to do anything other than accept what you are told by the specialist is the 'best' way to do things. There are ways in which specialist providers learn to take advantage of the unsuspecting organization. If catering staff are on the company payroll, but managed by the catering specialist, the contractors may not do their utmost to ensure that efficient staff are hired, that overtime is paid only when it is essential, that staff costs are minimized while efficiency is maximized. Similar problems can arise with the purchase of raw materials. There is little incentive to ensure that the best quality is bought for the lowest price if the bill is paid by the office organization, with a percentage handling fee for the caterers. This sort of problem can arise in connection with any contract with an outside service. Keeping up to date, staying on top of the cost consequences, become more necessary and more difficult. Ways can be devised to combat the problem, though they need continual monitoring and updating. As an example, Volvo in Sweden obtains office stationery through an outside provider who runs a 'shop' within the office as an alternative to a company-run stationery cupboard. The contract demands a regular reduction in supply costs, which gives an incentive to the provider to bring best-value opportunities to the notice of the company.

Catering

Even in an imperfect situation, the problem of managing an out-of-house catering company, which takes full responsibility for the kitchen and its output, may still be less burdensome than dealing with the proliferation of DIY coffee clubs that may be the alternative. A high electrical bill, trailing kettle leads, desk drawers full of coffee jars and biscuit crumbs, inter-departmental fights over which cupboard in the kitchen belongs to whom, whose milk is off in the fridge and why the sink is never wiped clean, the drifting aroma of chips or curry as microwave cookers hum into action on every floor may disappear like snow on a warm spring day when an imaginative company runs vending and catering for the whole building. Or it may not. So what should you do?

Catering takes a bewildering number of forms, reflecting eating habits, fashion, social structures and food technology. The triptych of an executive dining room, a management dining room and a staff canteen, reflecting the industrial origins of on-site catering, has been replaced in most organizations by a single cafeteria. This attempt at equality and social mixing, which is supposed to bring with it the benefits of communication, camaraderie and company loyalty, is often side-stepped by the provision of visitor dining facilities that are used by senior staff for eating-meetings – that is, when they don't arrange to wine and dine an important visitor at the best local restaurant. An advantage of city locations is that they offer people a wide range of possibilities for lunches, from cheap take-away sandwiches to exotic foreign cuisine or pub food. When a staff restaurant is provided, the feel of the place should be carefully considered. A complete change in lighting, colour scheme and general atmosphere is relaxing and provides more of a break from office routine than dining under the same lights and looking at the same interior design 'package' as on the office floor.

A publishing company created in its basement an entire pub assembled from elements of London pubs damaged in the Second World War, which provided an extremely popular lunch venue for both staff and clients.

If you are feeling peckish when in a large hotel, you may have the choice of making a cup of tea or using the minibar in your room, munching a quick snack from the functional cafeteria or dining lavishly in one of several different restaurants with varied decor before retiring to the lounge for coffee. In some office buildings the range is almost as extensive. In the SAS headquarters outside Stockholm staff may relax with a sandwich in their own group lounge, enjoy an *espresso* coffee and snack in the café on the main covered 'street', sit under a large garden umbrella on an informal balcony overlooking the street or go to one of two restaurants, with different menus, overlooking the lake. In the main restaurant they can choose to settle down by the fire in the warmed room or sit under the ivy in the conservatory. Are any of these choices available in your office building? Should they be?

How much to provide, what is essential, what impact an amenity has on staff, to what extent coffee is free to all staff – all are questions specific to each organization, to be answered in the context of its history and location. The personnel department (often known as 'human resources') is likely to have opinions and knowledge about these matters. Questionnaires can be used to tap staff opinion. As far as a building is concerned, the implications of making different sorts of provision that should be taken into account include:

- different space requirements for different types of catering, ranging between about 1 and 4 square metres per seat, including kitchen and serving areas
- overall space needed to cater for different numbers of staff – area per seat in serving area only, multiplied by the number of people per sitting
- the possibility of several sittings over a longer lunch period, which requires a smaller area
- the space-saving possibility of cashless transactions via smart cards or similar gadgets, reducing queues at the till
- hygiene rules for preparation and waste
- control of water contamination in kitchen areas, vending and water-cooling machines
- finishes and cleaning in catering areas – relative costs, suitable specifications
- the increase in average space per person if catering facilities are installed

- the impact on energy costs and the advisability of separate metering
- suitable location of kitchen extract, away from windows and ventilation air intakes.

The disabled: amenity becomes the standard

The needs of the disabled are many. There is a tendency to equate 'disabled' with 'in a wheelchair'. Without suitable ramps and door widths a person in a wheelchair cannot even get inside a building. The blind and partially sighted, those with reduced mobility or reach, the deaf and those with hearing difficulties, epileptics – all can often climb stairs and use ordinary doors. But their needs are not served if they cannot see the numbers on the lift buttons, or use a normal telephone, or get into a lavatory cubicle and use it unaided. These and other failures of provision mean that their ability to use office buildings can be seriously impeded.

Provision for the disabled in buildings is no longer simply a refinement provided by the philanthropically minded. In most countries it is now a requirement that new buildings meet some, though by no means all, of the needs of disabled people. In the first instance, access has to be suitable, with level changes provided with ramps, and doors that are sufficiently wide and easy to negotiate to enable people in wheelchairs to enter and to move around the building. A large lavatory cubicle is not a discretionary luxury. There must be at least one, with suitable support rails, in any new office building. This bears no relation to the likelihood of there being a disabled employee who needs this particular form of assistance, as statistically this is comparatively unlikely. Minimum provision is not enough if it blocks equality of opportunity: what was once considered an amenity has become a standard. While the new concern is an important step forward, the measures adopted must be assessed in relation to the benefits achieved. New provision must meet the standards, but upgrading substandard buildings is sometimes a poor use of resources. Taxis provide an example. To insist on full conversion of all the existing hackneys would be impractical, though requiring new taxis to be appropriately designed is an undoubted benefit to wheelchair users. Some, though not all, building features are similar. If necessary, an escort could help a disabled user confronting an inadequate lift, but front doors are another matter. If a person cannot get into the building at all, then changes must be made.

The significant issue in providing for the disabled is to appreciate that their needs must be met in a precise way. Perhaps the most generalizable difference between people with some level of disability and those without is the greater difficulty experienced by the former in adapting to a wide range of physical circumstances. A comparatively small variation from the ideal (say, in the height of a door handle) may not be noticed by a person who is able to bend, stretch and twist, whereas it can make things impossible for someone without full mobility.

There are some common mistakes in the design of office buildings that make access difficult and need constant vigilance if they are to be avoided. These include:

- doors that are too heavy
- ramps with slippery surfaces, no handrails and inadequate landings
- reception counters that are too high for wheelchair users to be seen or that have no induction loops for the hard of hearing
- lobbies and landings where door swings interfere with manoeuvring a wheelchair
- WC cubicles with some or many details incorrect
- light switches that are inaccessible or not in an intuitively sensible place
- lifts without a voice indicator or Braille buttons
- fire alarms with no visual signal
- vending areas and kitchens with controls that are too high
- no suitable furniture or spaces in waiting or meeting rooms.

Smoking rooms

Medicine's best-publicized research has established the dangers to health caused by smoking. Passive smoking has put the final nail into the coffin of equality of opportunity for those who feel they need to smoke or have a right to smoke wherever or whenever they wish. Smoking is a subject that arouses passions. Smokers feel that restrictions on their freedom to smoke where and when they like is an infringement of their civil liberties. Non-smokers behave as if they were narrowly escaping premature death by enforcing restrictions rigorously.

The duty, under the health and safety regulations, to provide staff with a healthy environment is now usually interpreted as meaning that it is essential to have a smoking room or a no-smoking policy. Many organizations, public and private, already have a 'smoking policy' (the usual name for a non-smoking policy) or at least expect to formulate and implement one soon. In fewer and fewer buildings is smoking freely permitted in all parts. Lifts and corridors, canteens and coffee lounges have all gradually become out of bounds to the cigarette. Even smoking in individual offices is not permitted by many organizations, as it sets an example they prefer not to endorse. Controlling smoke in places shared by smokers and non-smokers is harder than confining the problem to a few locations used only by smokers. This means that a room for people to retire to for a smoke must be provided in convenient locations, unless the company decides not to allow any smoking except outside the building.

The ventilation and decor of smoking rooms have, to date, not been given the attention they need and deserve. The surfaces rapidly become dingy, impregnated and discoloured by smoke. Yet without these rooms, however miserable the environment that they offer, some of the people in many offices are convinced that they could not do an effective day's work. How far this is true is not at issue. The decision to provide for smokers' needs may be the result of the fact that the chief executive smokes, the international policy of the organization, the need to set a health-conscious example or fashion. In a few more years the way in which employment offers and contracts are made may make the need for smokers' rooms unnecessary. Today what is needed is to be sure that smokers' rooms are properly located, designed and cleaned. Floors and wall finishes should be easily cleanable and need to have a more stringent cleaning regime than the rest of the office. Ashtrays should be large and need frequent emptying. Soft furniture should have removable covers that are regulary cleaned. It is a poor solution to provide vinyl chairs so that they can be wiped clean. They create an impression of a 'poor-relation' environment and are often difficult to keep looking good.

Smoking rooms, by their nature, smell like a noxious kipper factory, and the smell percolates rapidly into adjacent circulation routes and beyond. A lobby can help to solve this problem to a certain extent, but it is important to reduce the concentration of smoke in the room. A window that can be opened is inadequate to ensure that smoke is dissipated. Ventilation requirements are high, so use sufficiently powerful and adequately sized extract systems. Smokers are no keener than anyone else to freeze on a winter day. Whereas the recommended rate of fresh-air change in an office is 8 litres per second per person, this needs to be doubled if smoking is allowed, so in an office without a smoking ban 16 litres per second per person of fresh air is needed. With heavy smoking, as in a smoking room, this has to be doubled again, to 32 litres per second per person. A ventilation system is not an unmixed blessing. Without vigilance it sends the smoke, by indirect but effective routes, to the smoke-free zones in the rest of the office. Poor plant and duct maintenance, inappropriate locations for air outlets and intakes and incorrectly balanced systems can create this sort of problem, pleasing no one at all. This high fresh-air change rate leads, of course, to higher costs in heating (or cooling) the air. On top of this, a high rate produces a noticeable draught and a noise. There has been some American research that suggests even these levels are inadequate to reduce the likelihood of death from passive smoking to an acceptable minimum. To ensure that not more than one death occurs per 100,000 non-smokers over a forty-year working life would require three hundred times the normal rate of air change or prohibitively expensive air filtration. Neither of these approaches is relevant as they are so costly.

Car parking

> Q: 'What are the main problems that you have with this building?'
> A: 'The biggest issue right now is car parking.'
>
> Discussion between users and consultant prior to replanning their building
>
> 'The managing director gets a car-parking space whenever he wants, but we workers do not have the right to one even if we need it.'
>
> Comment by a city-centre office worker

Car parking is one of the most emotive issues in office management. As internal space within the office is gradually being made more equal, parking is a lingering area where status is still made absolutely clear. In the choice of a new office location senior management is more likely to reject one with insufficient car spaces for its perceived need than one with poorly designed spaces or low specification. In some organizations parking spaces are provided only for key workers whose jobs require the use of a car. But if offices are located at a distance from public transport, many people cannot get to work without the use of a car, even if their private transport then spends all day sitting in the car park. If spaces are allocated to specific individuals others grow frustrated in seeing empty spaces while they are unable to park. The outcry when spaces are reduced is loud, the deprivation heartfelt. Car parking takes up a great deal of space, so it is not surprising that status helps to decide who gets it. Each car requires 20 square metres for its bay and its share of the space to manoeuvre into and around the car park, which puts it on a level with an average of 15–20 square metres lettable area per person in a typical office. To provide this space is costly, whether in a basement area or outside the building. It needs lighting and security, and if it is outside, it should have some planting to mitigate the impression of a sea of tarmac.

It is hard to satisfy everyone. Car parking may be needed for staff, for visitors and for deliveries. At some times of the year there is more pressure on this scarce resource than at others. In November and December there are usually more people in the office than in other months – few people are away on holiday, as it is too late for autumn breaks and too early for skiing. The sizes of marked bays never match the size of cars. If the car park is underground, the columns, designed to suit the spaces above, never fit the circulation and parking requirements. If it is outside, spaces are often generous enough for the directors' limousines, so cars at the economical end of the range are swimming in space. Office users tend to want as many spaces as there are people. In urban areas planning officials may prevent them having any at all. Public transport needs to be excellent for this strategy to contain the spread of cars without generating apoplexy among commuters. It rarely is. Even in suburban areas users may not be allowed as many spaces as they would wish, although in some suburban office developments a larger area of ground is covered by car parking than by buildings, an unattractive sight without landscaping. In a more environmentally conscious world it is important to consider forfeiting a few car spaces for bicycle parking, ideally under cover and designed to permit secure locking.

Loos and lockers

Necessities, not discretional amenities – the quality of these areas says much about an organization and its landlord. Washrooms can be sumptuous or dirty and unloved, poorly designed or a pleasure to use. Their design should acknowledge the social role such spaces may play – for example, during the informal chat at meeting breaks. International research by a multinational company providing washroom services found high levels of user dissatisfaction with washrooms, particularly with their lack of cleanliness. In many organizations, to the great annoyance of staff, visitors' washrooms were better than those for staff. UK standards fell below those in Europe and North America. The environment matters: toilet areas must be clean, should smell pleasant, yet not too strong, and they should be well ventilated. In some office buildings management has chosen to add pleasing little touches more common in luxury hotels – boxes of disposable tissues, a clothes brush for grooming, a small vase of flowers, a comfortable easy chair.

Fashion, culture and budget dictate the details. In Scandinavia each cubicle is a complete room with solid, soundproof walls, its own light switch, basin, mirror and lavatory. In the UK it is more usual to find cheap and flimsy partitions between cubicles and an open-plan basin area. Partitions that reach neither the floor nor the ceiling are cheap to install, allow simple floor cleaning and make it easy to rescue someone who is locked in. They are less private than full-height ones and un-attractive to many users. There has been a succession of ideas about the most hygienic type of hand-washing and drying devices. 'No-touch' is now believed to be cleanest – electronic beams that start the water spray or the hot air when broken by your hands. They may be preferable to taps left permanently dribbling, or drifts of scrunched-up buff paper towels that run out when you need them, or continuous rolls of laundered fabric towelling, but they may also end up as some more pieces of equipment to go wrong. The design of washrooms needs to be carried out with their management in mind. If an outside specialist cleaner cares for them, and maintains all systems in sparkling order, then elaborate equipment may help to keep standards high. If not, simpler things may be preferable.

WC areas are usually designed differently for men and for women, which means estimating the likely sex balance of the occupant popula-tion or building an excess to allow for any mix from all males to all females. Equal opportunity of employment has its effect here. To avoid overprovision some companies now specify identical areas, with no urinals, so that they can be used for either group depending on the numbers of staff involved. Unisex WCs for the disabled are considered appropriate so there is no reason why the same principle should not be applied for all.

In some companies lockers are needed for people who have to change into uniform, such as receptionists, bank tellers, airline staff or security teams. People grow very attached to their lockers, and like them to be as large as possible, with generous space for changing near by. This can be at odds with efficient space use, and there is a trend, abetted by increasing commuting by car, towards encouraging people to travel to work in their uniforms. Where lockers are needed, they can be provided in one unisex space with individual changing cubicles or separate changing space for men and women. With areas for physical fitness creeping into office buildings, more rather than fewer lockers are needed.

Gyms and fitness rooms

The health of the workforce has always been a concern of employers. First-aid rooms for people who are injured or feeling ill and occupational health suites, where medical checks are carried out, have not completely disappeared. They are, however, being replaced by spaces for active physical exercise, now widely recognized as important for promoting health. Gyms and fitness rooms are often provided in larger buildings; even a small area can accommodate an extensive range of equipment. There are indications, from some companies' experience, that the overall health of staff can be improved by them, and the space devoted to a facility amply repays its cost. Some companies have agreed with the local council to allow public use of the gym when the staff do not use it, or have been paid by people outside the company for its use.

The design of a gym is a subject for a specialist, who should also be asked to advise on the legal requirements and the best management practices. Safety issues must be taken into account. For example, it is good practice to insist that fitness checks are carried out by a qualified doctor on prospective users and that a minimum of two people use the facility at any time in case of injury to one of them. There is a need for additional ventilation in gyms, showers and changing areas near by. If the office population is small, there need be no objection to showers that can be used by anyone, although privacy of changing within the cubicle must then be provided. Even where no gym or fitness room is included in a building, the provision of showers, mandatory in some countries, should be considered. They will be well received by those who bicycle to work and by joggers and will be used if general sessions of keep-fit, aerobics or self-defence are held on occasion in spaces such as the canteen or restaurant.

A high-quality, attractive environment

However many facilities are provided, however generous the space allowances, these are not the only ingredients of a high-quality, attractive environment. Good wall and floor finishes, well-built furniture and a cheerful colour scheme all contribute. Signs, door handles and all the other little details in the building need to be coordinated for the overall effect to be high-quality. Environmental psychologists find that the small, cheap, changeable items close to people are often the things that matter most – a colourful, elegant letter tray, pen holder or waste basket, used many times daily, is appreciated. Finishing touches are often provided by green plants and flowers and by artwork. A small percentage of the project budget can work miracles – '1 per cent art' is a goal of the artistic community, but even one hundredth of this can go a long way.

Plants in buildings have been in fashion since *Bürolandschaft* days. There are different management strategies for providing plants. None is intrinsically more 'right' than another, but they all demand different things of the building, different provision of floor space and ledges on which to put the plants, shorter or longer routes to fetch water, different hazards for the plants to encounter as they grow. One approach seeks a dramatic impact in central and public areas: the 6-metre-tall bamboo grove in the atrium, the forty-year-old palm tree brushing the receptionist's collar. In some buildings this is taken further to encompass a landscaped area with waterfalls, Japanese pebble gardens or cascades of creepers inside atria, on top of roofs and clinging to façades, with special lighting to help them grow and show them off to good effect. A different approach provides smaller plants around the entire office, so that everyone, wherever they are sitting, has some greenery to look at. This may be less impressive for the visitor but is more fun for the staff, who can observe the emerging new shoot, the unfurling leaf of 'their' plant. At the DIY end of the scale is the encouragement, or at least passive acceptance, of anyone and everyone bringing their own pots from home. The resulting jumble of variegated greenery can be charming or messy. It needs more care to create a specific effect – plants wither over the summer holidays, floods from overfilled saucers are likely, tendrils twine themselves where they are not wanted – but it has the merit that the plants belong to, and are tended by, people who care, and consequently they give real pleasure. The first two strategies require the services of a plant-maintenance company to select and tend the plants on a regular basis, feed them, shower and shine their leaves and retire them to more hospitable climes when the office environment causes droop, replacing them with bright young things. Such services can be excellent but come with a hefty price tag. Surely, says the finance controller, greenery can be bought for less money? Enter plastic and silk. The myth is that artificial plants have the same appeal but are maintenance-free. They do not, and they are not. They collect dust, look grimy and never attract the same allegiance from staff.

Where outside spaces are provided, such as courtyards, ornamental ponds or lakes and roof terraces, they should be made accessible to staff to offer the benefits of fresh air and opportunities for meeting or sitting outside on fine days. To plan them in such a way as to prevent this is foolish and unnecessary. The best locations are adjacent to the staff lounges or cafeterias or the reception and waiting areas.

Artwork, paintings, wall hangings, banners and sculpture are an easier source of quality than plants. They do not have the same maintenance cost; they are not killed off by unexpected downdraughts or blighted by an unchecked attack of red spider mite. They can also be modestly priced, and there is every reason to seek the quality and interest that they can bring to a building. In some organizations they are viewed as an important corporate investment that will appreciate in capital value, that can be shown off to visitors in reception areas, that may grace the lavish conference facility to impress customers or be hung on the executive floor. Your organization needs to be clear about whether its strategy is art for the bosses, art for the investors or art for the workers. Building design and layout must take account of the positions such items will occupy, and in some instances particular items may be commissioned to occupy especially prominent places. Business galleries rent out pictures and other artworks, so that they can be changed from time to time if you prefer not to commit your offices to a particular style over a long period. Remember that extra security and insurance may be needed for special items.

The green agenda

Staff are increasingly demanding an office organization that demonstrates that it cares about the environment. This demand is not unlike the demand for an amenity of any other kind. Governments can also put pressure on organizations, through taxes, fines or financial incentives, to behave in a more environmentally responsible way. They can affect location very powerfully in this way. Other changes that can be implemented to make an office more environmentally friendly are to do with building design or internal management. From surveys it seems that even these, closer to home, are not very likely to come from within. Managers have shown a limited commitment to energy-saving policies and, sadly, an even more limited one to the green agenda. This stance is influenced by the fact that there are few, if any, significant cost savings in going green except those associated with energy saving. The basic principles are to avoid waste, to reuse and recycle wherever possible, not to deplete irreplaceable or slowly replenished natural resources such a tropical hardwood, to minimize the production of pollutants and the exposure of staff to them. In numerous areas of building management this type of responsible approach may be no more difficult or costly than the way things were done before. There is scope in the office for the collection of used paper and the purchase of recycled stationery. Furniture and cleaning products can also be purchased in a responsible way. Equipment such as photocopiers, printers and computers can be chosen and sited with good practice in mind and care taken to avoid toxic materials and to promote the safe handling of any chemicals used. In the catering field the provision of a balanced diet, safe waste disposal, including composting of appropriate food wastes, the recycling of glass and tin, washable rather than disposable utensils and the avoidance of styrofoam blown with CFCs are all to be recommended.

All these are small contributions to the solution of a big problem. This does not invalidate them, but a bigger impact can be made in other ways. When new buildings or large renovation projects are undertaken, there is an opportunity to make environmentally sound decisions in a number of areas. Reusing rather than replacing buildings and furniture is less wasteful in many situations. Adopting a sane attitude to location, allied to a suitable national policy on transport, is vital. Saving energy by care in building design can make its contribution. Savings in lighting, heating and cooling can be achieved by good window design, adequate insulation, external sun shading and tree planting to avoid excessive heat gain, well-planned ventilation and sensible, energy-efficient lighting installations. To pursue the green agenda, use every oportunity to make improvements as you make other building changes.

Summary

This chapter will help you to decide if your organization should provide special facilities beyond the working areas, which ones and to what quality. Office buildings offer a variety of facilities that are not designed directly to enable the work of the office to be carried out. These may be considered perks, additional amenities making the office a better place to work, or they may be thought of as essentials for the support of the office staff. Special leisure areas, cafeterias, a crèche can seem like a luxury, but for sites where local services are hard to access, or when change is introducing added stress, or when staff are hard to attract, they may become vital. Some facilities are a legal requirement.

There are disadvantages as well as advantages for management. The responsibilities that go with amenities must be taken into account. Kitchens have to be run according to strict food-hygiene legislation; sports facilities have to follow safety procedures. These responsibilities can be placed on someone else's shoulders. An amenity such as catering can be 'outsourced', given to a specialist company to run under contract. A disadvantage of outsourcing is that, once you shed the burden, you may lose the in-house expertise to evaluate services provided by others.

The requirement to provide for disabled access and use of buildings is an example of how what in the past may have been a 'luxury' provision, offered only by the richest companies, has become a necessity – a legal one as well as, hopefully, the response of a generation of caring companies. There is considerable emphasis on the requirements imposed by wheelchair access, but other forms of provision, for the large group of deaf, blind or partially sighted and partially mobile office workers and visitors, are no less important. Very heavy doors, highly polished floors, exclusively audible fire warnings and written instructions for safety or lift operation may present problems for non-wheelchair users.

Green agendas have been shown by researchers to be of little interest to management. They have been a major media issue, but collecting paper for recycling is about as far as most offices go. All consumables could be more rigorously treated; work and management practices could be tailored to a green agenda as well as immediate business requirements. This may come about only when pressure is brought to bear through centrally imposed incentives and penalties.

The overall quality of the environment is an important amenity. All the options suggested in this chapter are positive, whether included in the building as requirements for legal or work reasons or supplied in the spirit of providing an excellent workplace. Even if only small areas can be devoted to special facilities, they can be planned so that a range of activities can take place in them. Conference suites can accommodate classes after work; cafeterias can be equipped with stacking furniture so that they can be cleared for exercise groups or the Christmas party. These areas are more cost-effective if they can be well used throughout the day and the year.

Even an intelligent building can suffer from subsidence.

> **Q: What price the paperless office?**
> A: More paper.

The paperless office, the office of the future, is a promise to be brought about by the huge changes that information technology – IT – makes. New and glamorous ways to record, retrieve and transmit information are predicted. The office will come into its own, efficient as never before. These changes are brought about by rapidly falling prices of electronic equipment that started to have a serious impact in the early 1980s. There is a price to pay. As the cost of equipment went down, the cost of buildings rose with higher capital as well as maintenance and running costs. The buildings were filled with wires and heat-producing equipment. Everyone, or almost everyone, now has a computer on their desk, some special people have more than one, and all the other equipment like printers, faxes and copiers, are cheap enough to scatter throughout the office for convenient access. More space at the desk, more wires to be hidden, more air-conditioning means that low-specification buildings, particularly those built in the 1960s and 1970s, are unfitted to cope with this relentless march of progress.

Electronic equipment has truly revolutionized many of the ways in which people work and the assumptions that underpin the idea of the office. The developments in this field have been astonishing, exciting and productive. They permeate all office work today – even the most traditional types are affected somehow. The speed and extent of their impact was predicted, yet not understood until it happened.

The equipment proliferates

Many people have the creation and handling of knowledge as the core of their work. Some of this may not take place in offices, but increasingly the 'knowledge-based industries', as they have come to be described, have a large office-based component. Office work and offices have been transformed by access to key pieces of equipment at different historical stages, especially the telegraph, the typewriter and the telephone. Consider the typewriter. In 1873 Remington was looking for an outlet for precision instruments, as firearms, his speciality, were no longer in high demand after the end of the American Civil War. In 1879 fewer than 200 typewriters were sold, but by 1890 annual sales reached 65,000. The development of office buildings at this time was influenced by the need to house the large, low-paid, largely female labour force employed to use this equipment. The telephone too started as a specialized piece of equipment: maybe one or two in an organization. Tales of the days when there was only one in the entire British Foreign Office, located in a basement corridor, are still current. They may be apocryphal, but they are a reminder of how rapidly the telephone has spread. In the Foreign Office many desks have had several telephones for decades now. In most office buildings most people have access to one, normally on their own desk. It has changed the speed with which things are done; it has changed the distances over which they can be performed; it has transformed business life. Introducing telephones into offices was slightly more complicated than placing a typewriter on a desk, but not much more so, as the wires required are tiny, flexible and easily routed to almost anywhere. The equipment has shrunk a bit, but it was never very large. Miniature, portable and mobile telephones have extended the situations in which they can be used, but the major impact on office work came about by making them available to everyone on their desks.

With such precedents it is hardly surprising that the potential of information technology to generate great changes created such a stir as it entered the office in the 1970s and 1980s. As the office workforce had grown so dramatically, a great many people were going to be affected by the monumental changes. The spinning jenny appears to have had nothing on the computer in its capacity to cause vast and permanent changes in the working lives of millions. The first computers were very large, very expensive and could be used only by experts who understood them. They did not become common in office buildings until they had shrunk a little, and even then they still needed special rooms, with air-conditioning, and special people to look after the 'mainframes'. What a few people had on their desks then were 'dumb' terminals, able to perform only when connected to the mainframe. Mini-computers, no bigger than a family fridge and not requiring nearly so much space or such special conditions, were miniaturized versions of mainframes. They spread the computing habit to a wider range of users. The quantum leap occurred, however, when technical advances and further

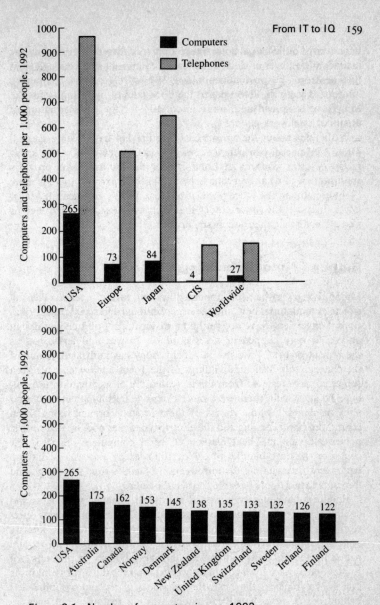

Figure 8.1   Number of computers in use, 1992.

Source: Karen P. and Egil Juliussen, *The 6th Annual Computer Industry Almanac 1993*, Reference Press, Inc., Austin, 1993, from figs. 12.2, 12.4, pp. 386–7.

miniaturization led to a powerful computer, cheap enough to buy for individual members of staff, in a piece of equipment small enough to fit on a desktop. The most influential was IBM's PC (personal computer), introduced in 1980. That opened the floodgates of opportunity for the equipment to spread and, more important, for the transformation of organizational work patterns.

Predictions about the spread of IT equipment have been exceeded. There are, indeed, computers on most desks. A survey of a particular group of office workers in London over the last ten years provides confirmation of what everyone believes, that year by year there is more IT in use among the office population, that VDUs are used for longer hours, that it is the lower grades that use them most, although there is also an increase in their use by senior staff.

Getting IT into the building

Major changes to be accommodated are still in the pipeline. The full effects of miniaturization, and the organizational and social transformations it engenders, have not yet had a major impact on building design or use. It may happen in a series of tiny waves and jerks, just as the impact of the IT we use in offices today has infiltrated. Many of the changes to which the buildings of the 1960s and 1970s have been subjected have resulted from the increased use of information technology. To start with, there were more extensive telephone networks and telex machines – whole rooms of them in some organizations. Then centralized photocopying and the electric typewriter pool needed rooms, power supplies and heat extracts. Central computers required new risers for the huge bundles of cables, followed by a spread of desktop equipment necessitating the introduction of cables routes cut into solid floors, in raised floors or cable trays in the ceilings.

Buildings have also been ripped apart and threaded with wires and equipment intended to control the building. Fire-alarm systems, electronically controlled boilers to deliver monitored temperatures, security systems, updated lighting with electronic control devices – all require routes for the wires, new equipment like lights, boilers, thermostats, not to mention a space for a computer workstation for the security man. As one system replaces the next, the remnants of the old are often left behind. Extra wires have been added without removing old ones, as they could not be easily reached, which makes it hard to know whether the old ones are connected to a vital piece of equipment, and gradually ducts have become clogged. It is surprising, after this treatment, that any of the buildings that were predicted to fail under the strain of the introduction of IT survived the experience at all. Some have found the strain too great. They stand unloved and empty or have been pulled down and replaced.

Space and furniture

As IT entered the office, the workforce felt invaded. Space was being given to machines at the expense of people. Amenity areas were taken over by computer rooms. Desks were too crowded to work at comfortably. Unions representing office employees affected by these changes were distressed. Luddism prevailed. Afraid that people themselves might be put out of work, employees were often hostile to any introduction of equipment. The white-collar workforce continued to grow, despite union fears, and the struggle concentrated on ensuring that a good working environment would be maintained. The early equipment was, indeed, large and cumbersome, intrusive and space-hungry. The desks that had suited an earlier work style did become crowded, with little room for anything except the VDU terminal, and were rapidly buried in a tangle of cables. Breakthroughs came only as the equipment began to shrink. Other equipment has also proliferated: fax machines, answering machines, desktop copiers. The extra desks required for the IT are a factor to be taken into account when deciding how many desks are needed for a group of staff. Though equipment is small enough to fit on a desk, shared items need a place of their own, so that a procession of users does not disturb anyone too much. In an open plan arrangement there is often a convenient corner to place them. If the organization uses a series of small, enclosed offices, the equipment may end up in the corridor, unsupervised and abused, or someone has to share their office with it, and it becomes a burden for them to be disturbed constantly and a bore for others who wish to access it.

Changes in technology have taken place so fast that the furniture industry seems to have been left one step behind. To a complex problem a specific solution has been offered, but the problem has changed. Desk-based cable-management systems, created to hide and contain wires safely, are often more complicated than they need be. A basic, roomy basket hooked on under the desk may do a better job than cable routes needing fancy threading, cover strips and a built-in channel with an elaborate lid that turns out not to fit the socket extensions. Individual air-conditioning at the desks to cope with local heat gain has been made redundant by small equipment producing less heat. Special desks that accommodate clumsy keyboards at the best level for VDU users but do not suit tasks using pen and paper have been displaced by thinner keyboards and the universal desk that takes into consideration the new reality that anyone, anywhere may have a VDU but every desk must also work for people who do not. Mobile computer trolleys were useful where only a few computers were available to a large group, but increasingly organizations are able to afford one on every desk, so the trolleys have become redundant. Special multi-level printer tables with slots for continuously fed paper are being replaced in ordinary offices by small desktop laser or inkjet printers. There are organizations, such as the financial dealing houses, where up to six VDU screens appear on each desk. Special furniture has been created, like something out of *Star Trek*, so that everything can fit and be reached without causing an accident or missing a deal. Elsewhere advances in technology have reduced the six VDUs to a few with a 'split screen', a single screen functioning like several independent ones, with software that sometimes allows a single bit of equipment on a standard desk to carry out functions that previously needed several separate screens in a special console. Generally the simpler furniture solutions have fared better over time.

The terminal, VDU and keyboard have been joined on the desktop by so many gadgets that it is now usual to supply power and data to every desk and to make available four, six or in some cases even more socket outlets. While not every desk uses them all at any one time, the range of power-consuming equipment that may be placed on desks is huge, and the flexibility offered by ensuring that anything could, if necessary, be placed anywhere in the office is very valuable. There are the desktop printers – far too many of them in some places because cables to connect them in networks to a whole group of computers have not been used. Sometimes this is the result of the many different and incompatible pieces of equipment that burst on to the market in the early days. Different machines were marketed to do different tasks, and as the software was not interchangeable, there seemed to be as many makes and models as tasks. The different machines could not 'talk' to each other, so, among other problems, they could not share printers. This type of confusion has subsided; more of the bits of kit are now interchangeable or compatible. There is little excuse for a printer for each machine, one on every desk. Where this still occurs steps should be taken to link several to a single conveniently located printer.

Larger equipment in special rooms has not disappeared just because there is more equipment all over the office. Mainframe and larger-computer suites are still needed by some organizations, and these still need raised floors, temperature and humidity controls, a dust-free environment and special security control points. Some smaller organizations have computer rooms, maybe with ventilation and a raised floor, but they are not the laboratory type of environment staffed by high-level specialists of the early mainframe days. They are often more like warehouses-cum-workshops. New equipment delivered in boxes sits in piles on the floor, waiting to be checked and then installed on someone's desk; shelves are crowded with repair kits, broken modems, manuals and miscellaneous cables; and the file server hums and growls under the workbench. The most complicated copiers, printers or mailing machines, now electronically controlled, less noisy than in the past and smaller, are generally used only if they can serve the whole office, so they still get a separate room accessible to every department.

To date, as everyone knows, the paperless office is the bit of the science-fiction scenario that has not come about. Bearing in mind that it takes ten years for a tried and proven technological development to be turned into usable and affordable machines, the spread of desktop and general office electronic equipment has been as rapid as most of the intelligent predictions of the early 1980s suggested. The range of tasks, the ingenuity with which these have been combined into multifunction machines, the speed and power that can be afforded in desk-based equipment have all come up to expectation. At the same time the manufacturers of paper filing systems have expanded their ranges, streamlined their products and moved in for the kill. The Swedish paper industry has doubled its worldwide production in the last decade. The new machines have made it possible to generate vastly more paper ever more rapidly; multiple drafts are so easy to create and meeting minutes can be easily photocopied and automatically stapled straight from the wordprocessor. If the new equipment has permitted some reduction in paper – 'hard copy', as the IT jargon now demands it to be called – this has merely served to keep things in roughly the same place. At the same time computers have raised expectations about speed of retrieval. No wonder high-density filing, described in detail in chapter 5, is creeping (or rather, lumbering, as it is bulky stuff) into more and more offices.

If the IT industry has its way, this could be another example of the furniture industry getting its act together just in time for obsolescence. Electronic filing is getting closer to becoming an affordable technology. There have been a number of attempts to miniaturize paper records. Microfilming and microfiche systems have been adopted by some organizations. These have involved expensive photographic sessions and the use of bulky microfiche readers that are too specialized to perform any function other than to provide a hard-to-read version of a document that cannot be taken back to the desk. Methods to capture documents on computers are also becoming more affordable. Optical character reading, advances in equipment that can read varieties of handwriting and electronic storage on laser disks with fast retrieval systems are all coming together to make it possible that far more files will soon be kept in purely electronic form. Large insurance companies and building societies are among the groups to have invested in such electronic storage and to have reaped enormous gains from it. The potential market for such storage is vast and will be exploited in the next decade as electronic storage grows cheaper. Then some of the rotary filing units described in chapter 5 may not be wanted after all. If people can be prevented from overworking the printer, some of the stationery cupboard can go as well. The in tray, fax machines and a good part of the mail room will vanish when e-mail is widely used and memos and messages can be sent around the office, or around the world, at the press of a key on the desktop PC.

Cables, heat and noise

The unexpected burden of paper storage and possible electronic solutions is a digression. No one anticipated that the price of the paperless office was to be more paper-storage equipment. It was going to be cables and heat. Well, that prediction has come true, though not always in the way that was imagined. The first companies to invest in desktop equipment for large numbers of staff were swamped in tangles of wires. Cables were seen lying on the floor, sometimes taped down to ensure passive behaviour, wandering down corridors and disappearing into holes in walls, crawling over desks and leaping gaps between wall sockets and the computers. A serious danger to safety, the cables had to be controlled. At this point the furniture manufacturers homed in on a potential selling point and invented 'cable management'. They rapidly developed desks that take care of all the cables, and, if you pay enough, also provide air conditioning.

Even if the desk can subdue the cables once they reach it, there is still the problem of getting the cables there. Providing socket outlets near the desk is thus a priority. Creating routes around office buildings for cables has been a major preoccupation. The question is how to get traditional cables around the building and equally important, how to alter them as people move or their requirements change. Small buildings or highly cellularized ones have managed perfectly well with cables buried in walls, partitions or columns, or running round the floor at the edge of the building. If a great deal of equipment is needed, the cable-route problem can be solved by trunking, into which socket outlets can be fitted as often as required. Prairie farming has created huge fields, great for tractors but with no hedgerows for wild-life habitats and hiding places. Deep or medium open plan offices have stripped away walls, the normal hiding places for socket outlets near each desk. Many 1960s buildings were built with small cable trays in their concrete floor screeds to bring socket outlets to the middle of open office floors. Some of these could take only two sorts of cable and only in small amounts. Drilling out extra or bigger routes took place time after time as equipment poured into these buildings. Electrical track with almost no thickness, cunningly laid under carpets, did not provide the ultimate solution. The need to handle three kinds of wire, power, data and telecom (even though that is really only another form of data), means that crossover points, and changes in one but not the others, are more easily dealt with using more traditional wiring technologies. A raised floor – that is, a second floor that is supported on masses of tiny legs, or on strips of wood, to provide a surface to walk on that is above a structural floor – had been a feature of mainframe computer rooms. Here they could be up to 1 metre above the structural floor. During the 1980s these became commonplace in ordinary office areas, though very much shallower. A few bold office designers in the UK followed some European and North American examples and chose to use the ceilings as a distribution plane and to bring cables down from above. To get cables under the floors or above the ceilings in the first place means that big bundles of them have to be carried up vertical ducts from the main switches. Sometimes the bundle is as thick as the torso of a body-building fanatic. New ducts have had to be cut into the concrete floors of old buildings, as the ones they were built with were too small. These are some of the reasons why the offices of the 1960s and 1970s did not measure up to the demands of the IT revolution. There is not enough floor to ceiling height in many of them to insert raised floors and no efficient way of adding the vertical ducts to carry the cables around. Buildings were, and often still are, built with low ceilings, partly in an attempt to cram as many floors as possible into them, within imposed height restrictions, and partly because heating tall rooms is an extravagance office occupiers are keen to avoid. Older buildings have often fared better, as they started with more generous dimensions.

The cables have not gone away. Some of them will stay whatever happens. Fibre-optic links and cordless links have not replaced them yet, though for some functions these are now being used. Fibre-optic cable may be useful where large capacity on a simple route is required, but it is far from being a panacea. It suffers from high cost, jointing problems and a requirement for a wide bending curve, and it needs protection throughout. Cordless systems using radio and microwave bands or infrared light are also expensive and only support slower transmissions, so they are less appealing for transmitting large volumes of data. None the less, these technologies are well suited to specific tasks. Infrared beams, which are use in most homes with a television set in the form of a remote control unit, can easily be put to use in switching lights on and off. For example, a system designed to control electricity costs, which switches all the lights off in an open plan office by means of a simple time switch, can also be equipped with an infrared remote-control system allowing individuals to switch 'their' lights on if they need to.

More important is the fact that people are gradually understanding the problem – the proliferation of cables, the reluctance to pull out obsolete cables when alterations are made, the number that people need and where they want them. So places to put them and sensible patterns in which to lay them are being devised. Structured cabling is one such: a tree type of distribution is used with a main trunk to all floors, big branches to convenient switching points and twigs that can be removed and re-attached at these points to connect specific outlets to the tree. Structured cabling reduces the need for miles of cable and allows for cost-effective rerouting, so it is a sensible expedient for many reasons. A new system for data handling is emerging that uses twisted copper wires like those of telephone technology but of a heavier variety. Without the phenomenal capacity of fibre-optic cable, it has a number of substantial advantages. It is far cheaper to install, is less temperamental and has no need for special devices at the ends to connect it to the rest of the system. Short lengths work best, so it relies on the continued development of structured cabling. Other problems have not yet been solved. The provision of both raised floors and lowered ceilings in a building may be overspecification. Funding institutions still expect raised floors, and cheap lighting systems popular with developers are often integrated into suspended ceilings, so many overspecified properties are around or still being built. Pressure must be exerted by users to change the mindset of the funding institutions.

Equipment has shrunk faster than was considered likely. Smaller equipment has reduced cable requirements and, more dramatically, heat loads. All things being equal, smaller equipment creates less heat. The typical equipment ratings on the manufacturers' metal plate at the back, where only the technical team ever look, are cautious and tend to give a higher rate of expected heat output than is found in reality if the equipment is tested. Naturally the manufacturers' figures are believed, as they are usually the only ones available, but the actual load is often smaller than planned for – about a third the amount is typical. The discrepancy went unnoticed at first, as the rate at which the use of equipment would expand was underestimated. There was a lot more equipment than had been predicted, so the overall heat output was more or less as expected, or at least not noticeably lower. It could be extremely uncomfortable in some types of office (dealing rooms are an obvious example) if there is no extra ventilation or air-conditioning. Today heat from small equipment is not quite the problem that it once was, but it must not be forgotten. On the contrary, it must be sensibly taken into account when planning how to design and run an office building. For example, rather than being an unwanted burden, the heat from both equipment and lights should be regarded as part of the heating system and used positively.

Noise has crept in alongside some of the equipment. Advances in technology tended to produce noisy intrusion, which has vanished as further improvements have been made. Typewriter pools used to be pretty noisy places; modern keyboards produce a gentler sound. Early dot-matrix printers clattered loudly, even under those ugly hoods, whereas ink-jets and lasers merely swish. Developments in telephone systems have silenced the incessant rings. You can be found by a follow-me system, or a message can be radioed to your pocket bleeper, so your neighbours next to your empty desk are no longer obliged to block their ears to shut out the bell. The next noise frontier of concern is voice-activated computers, which are already entering the office.

Energy efficiency

If they are uneconomic to keep, office buildings as we know them, even properly filled with the right equipment and activities, could disappear. One of the costs that could be reduced is expenditure on fuel. Buildings use a large proportion of the fuel we burn. In the UK 50 per cent of our energy consumption can be attributed to buildings. A large part of that is used in houses, hospitals and factories, but offices use enough to make a very sizeable impact on the country's consumption of finite resources and on pollution. A great deal of work has been done to demonstrate how energy is used in office buildings and how it can be reduced. Very little real effect has yet been seen in changed management decisions, although the design professions are trying hard to incorporate some of the research insights into buildings and systems. Despite all manner of publicity programmes, saving energy is still low on the business agenda. It should not be. Saving costs means higher profits; efficiently designed and managed systems are the best defence against rising costs for the future. Saving energy and reducing pollution are vital, in the longer term, for the whole population of the world. Even if the total effect on the nation's energy consumption can be affected only marginally by energy saving in all existing offices, this is no justification for ignoring the issue.

The UK Energy Efficiency Office with the help of the Building Research Establishment has published a series of best-practice guides that explain the most efficient approaches to energy use in offices through a series of real case studies. They identify four general types of office building. For each type the guide gives an average and a target for energy consumption and contrasts these with what can be achieved by good practice. There are some clear messages. Good-practice levels of consumption can save between 30 and 40 per cent of the cost per square metre of treated building (that is, excluding places like plant rooms and car parks). This is true whatever the type of building, whether naturally ventilated or air-conditioned. It is an amount well worth saving. The larger problem is more often electricity consumption than heating. Mainframe computer rooms use large amounts of electricity, of which some can be recouped if heat gains are recycled to where heating is required elsewhere in the building. If the building is air-conditioned, it is not the refrigeration that uses the most energy, but fans and pumps, so it is not the amount of cooling but the time it is in operation that most influences the cost. The expense of air-conditioning may be avoidable altogether. Chapter 6 examines the reasons for not

	£ million per square metre treated floor area (approx.)	
	Typical	Good practice
Prestige air-conditioned	21	15
Standard air-conditioned	14	8
Naturally ventilated open plan	8	5
Naturally ventilated cellular	6	4

Figure 8.2 Costs for energy consumption in office buildings, 1991.

Source: Energy Efficiency Office, DOE, *Energy Efficiency in Offices*, London, HMSO, 1994

having it where it is not essential. The saving of energy is another compelling reason to avoid the other problems it causes.

It all sounds straightforward. Why are the improvements fewer than they should be? Because managers do not know how easy it can be. To save energy you need good information. You must know about quantities of fuel used, areas in which systems operate and hours of operation for the different systems. Meters to check the amount and pattern of energy use are needed to collect this information, such as a meter for kitchens and computer suites or a meter to separate lighting costs from those of other power used. Even if they have to be installed especially, their cost can be recouped in energy saved. Lights are often the largest individual item among electrical costs, so work out what to do about them. It may be a simple matter of replacing those that are on for longest with up-to-date bulbs, reflectors and controls. If a totally new system is required to reduce consumption, there is an opportunity to create a more congenial working atmosphere. Bear in mind, though, that the total energy costs, including those of energy used in production of new equipment, are not really incorporated in the calculation of the pay-back period. What is good for your organization may not be good for the global use of energy.

Focus the management of energy on matching performance standards to real needs. In other words, do not run things when you do not need them. See that office equipment is not left on unnecessarily, especially overnight. Make sure that air-conditioning does not run longer than needed to keep the building at an acceptable temperature where and when people are actually working. If you are air-conditioning a computer suite, make sure that you keep separate records of the power running the computers and the power needed for the air-conditioning because if the air-conditioning is using more than 60 per cent of the amount of power needed to run the computers, it can probably be made more efficient.

Intelligent buildings or intelligent technicians?

How can a building possibly be described as intelligent? If it is, is it a wilful Frankenstein monster? Is it something the average office owner, renter or user wants to have, or should you fend it off with a bargepole? Our cut-throat culture prizes intelligence, so intelligent must be 'good'.

Intelligence, knowledge and feedback have all got muddled up in this handy portmanteau term. The Citroën car in the 1950s was one of the first consumer products to make use of the concept of feedback and response in machines. The relationship of the suspension to speed and to steering around corners was interactive. What was happening as a result of one had an effect on the behaviour of the others, and the driver could benefit from the feedback. Generally it is the possibilities inherent in the feedback of information, rather than any concepts of knowledge or intelligence, that are of importance in buildings. And the feedback will be only as good as the information it has to work on. An example of the way such feedback can be used is in ensuring that safety regulations are not breached. For a building where flexitime or hot desking is used, or where large meetings take place, maybe you need 'eyes' in the door frames to count people in and out, so that the security system 'knows' if exceptional attendance means that the occupancy of the building as a whole is approaching its limit for fire-evacuation purposes. This information could trigger a ban on additional people entering, just like a parking-garage system that says 'Full' at the entry gate. Few office buildings really have a need for this, so to provide it as an 'intelligent' feature would not make a lot of sense. This sort of gadgetry is not intrinsically desirable or intelligent. It is useful in specific, rather limited circumstances, but the problems must be framed by people, and the solutions must serve them.

The massive developments in electronic equipment over the last thirty years have attacked office buildings from two directions. The huge expansion in the use of computers in offices has been discussed above. From the other direction, electronics have been deployed in the systems that control different aspects of buildings – the heating and cooling systems, the lifts, the security and fire-alarm systems. As these have become more sophisticated they have been able to make a building behave a bit like that famous Citroën, to respond to more sensitive sets of needs, to work with feedback from the effects of the last thing that it did. Each of the systems in the building has been enhanced in different ways. Heating and ventilating systems can calculate optimum running patterns to achieve desired temperatures and air movement under different external and internal conditions. Lifts can do more than just respond to the first demand made on them; they can work out the optimum route for the calls demanded. Electronic security systems can report who has been past the most sensitive barriers, which is invaluable for an organization concerned to protect its products against industrial espionage. Fire-alarm systems can carry information about how many people are in a particular part of the building, or which sprinklers have been activated, and can flash instructions about evacuation during an emergency. Choosing a system that will offer the organization benefits that it needs, based on equipment that it can manage, is a specialist skill.

The controls of all these systems can be linked together through a single piece of equipment, so that what one is doing can be taken into account by the others. These are known as building management systems (BMS) or, if intended particularly to handle energy and fuel use, building energy management systems (BEMS). They enable effective fire-safety systems, complicated and specific security needs and elaborate heating and ventilation systems to be installed and run in large and complicated buildings. They are an important element in the energy-saving approaches discussed above. BEMS can send information and accept instructions about the systems under its control via a remote computer, even one in the chief engineer's home at the weekend and can permit more cost-effective and efficient monitoring and adjustment of the heating. In organizations with many buildings these systems can be especially helpful, as the remote reporting can lead to immediate action to reduce management costs.

Building management systems are frequently described as if they were an unalloyed benefit. They are if they have been designed to meet your needs and until they go wrong. They can also cost a lot to buy, and if they do not fulfil your organization's needs, the irritation that they can cause may not be worth the potential savings. Even a simple system may be too complicated for the job it is doing. A security system that cannot be explained to members of staff who work late has disadvantages that a simpler one would avoid. A CCTV in the car park and at the back door may be all that is needed. The significant issue is that many of these systems rely on cables. The routes that these take through the building need to be simple, accessible for maintenance and able to accept additions and changes. Introducing such cables has challenged older buildings but is becoming more standard in newer ones. None the less, if you need a security barrier at the car-park gate, which is to be opened by the receptionist pressing a button when someone authorized wishes to enter, a conduit is needed from the reception desk to the car-park gate. Do not leave it until the granite has been laid in the entrance hall and the car park has been surfaced before deciding that this is an important part of the receptionist's role. Otherwise you may have to settle for a wireless control system.

The idea of 'intelligent building' could have developed into a monster dreamed up by science-fiction writers exploring the limits of computer intelligence, a building so complex that humans would not be clever enough to disentagle all the interconnected parts and would have to rely on computers. Before it did, the idea mutated into something much more amorphous. It is currently couched in terms of responsiveness to user needs, able to service requirements with cables or heating systems or change partition layouts – whatever people decide they want. The human choice and instructions come first. The building is 'intelligent' if it is possible to carry out the instructions without tearing it apart, if the layout, construction and servicing systems have taken into account how different needs may play themselves out over time. This begs the question of what changes an 'intelligent' building can be expected to cope with. It is not possible to replan a long, thin building to work like a big, wide, open plan one or vice versa. Does that preclude buildings with definite shapes, better able to accommodate one type of layout than another, from ever being intelligent?

Rescue from the monster has not done away with the issue of whether the people running systems within a building really know enough to manage the more sophisticated products of engineering ingenuity. A bigger danger than an unintelligent, unresponsive building holding back your business is likely to be the difficulty or cost of employing technical staff able to understand and get the best out of even fairly simple systems. Better a familiar set of controls that anyone can understand and that needs regular but easy adjustment than something capable of making its own sequence of adjustments but demanding an engineering degree to understand the manual and maintain the system at peak efficiency. If such a system is working inefficiently, the consequences may be unexpectedly expensive.

Future technology

Technology is moving fast. It is important to stay alert for developments, as there will undoubtedly be useful as well as hopeless equipment. 'Microchips with everything' is not intrinsically good, but it is a reality to be taken seriously. The specialists are not always easy to communicate with. The field does move fast, so it is tempting to believe – or, possibly more accurately, hard to deny – someone who says, 'I must have this', as it is not easy to really know what 'this' is. Some developments will be just gadgets; others will represent major changes, leaps forward. Each jump in technology in the past – the typewriter, the telephone, the desktop computer and now the Internet – has been allied to a change in the way knowledge-based work has been done. The costs of the technology are still in free fall, to which there is as yet no apparent end. Technology changes have been reflected in the buildings. Further changes will alter how people work, what they need and expect of their buildings.

Summary

This chapter helps you to understand the impact on office buildings of the rapid changes in information technology used for office work. It alerts you to changes still to come.

As IT has continued to develop and spread, many claims have been made on its behalf. One, that computers heralded an era in which the office could function with less or even no paper, has manifestly been shown to be untrue. The effects that IT has had – to multiply manyfold the cables that need to be accommodated and to create heat – have, on the other hand, bulked large in people's minds, partly because they were not expected. Cables are gradually becoming less of a problem. Structured cabling greatly simplifies rerouting, without the necessity to run new links. Radio transmission of voice or data eliminates the cables entirely. Heat is not so hot as was thought either. Smaller equipment and more realistic assessments of actual output are cutting the problem down to size. But cabling still needs to be taken into account when ventilation systems and office layouts are planned.

Energy efficiency has been championed by governments for a long time. In the UK, for example, this policy is backed up by excellent information, with comparatively poor results. The cost savings that are the prime incentive are apparently proportionately too low to be of interest to management. Energy saving needs to concentrate on well-designed lighting, no unnecessary air-conditioning, well-insulated buildings, excellent plant management and maintenance.

'Intelligent buildings' have become a new focus for interest. These are not simple buildings with well-planned and efficiently managed services using a BEMS or with a computer on every desk. If the term is usefully applied, it indicates that the full powers of computing technology can be used to help create a building in which the users' needs trigger suitable responses.

It is vital that whatever the systems installed in a building, whether computer-controlled or not, there are suitable people available to run them. A simple system with little responsiveness and few subtleties, which can be run by the janitor on a part-time basis, may be preferable to one that never works as it was designed to because no one understands how to make that happen.

Providing for the IT needs of a company is usually challenging and will, for the foreseeable future, require a high degree of alertness.

9 Over to You: All Change

Over to you

So where has all this been leading? What can you do with all these ideas? Do they really apply to your office building? The organization in which you work may be a bank, a university department, a 'clerical factory' back office, a manufacturing head office, a legal consultancy, a government department, the administration arm of a museum, hospital or factory. Each one is different, with specific requirements, experiences and opportunities. Yet they are all offices. The material in this book covers a range of information about offices couched in general terms. The intention has been to equip managers – you – with the type of information that will enable you to look critically at your present office building or a proposed new one, your specialist advisers and your internal building-management procedures and to uncover ways to create a pleasant environment, promote your business and increase staff morale and productivity, as well as saving money, making better use of your building, and avoiding unnecessary or inappropriate actions and pitfalls.

The moment when all the questions about buildings urgently need answers is when major changes are planned, such as relocation to new premises or the renovation of existing buildings. This is the ideal opportunity to reap the benefits of understanding your office space.

Should you move?

A manager may be less aware of the impact of inadequate space than others in the organization. Managers, after all, usually manage the business, not the building. They are often kept remote from the worst effects of spatial problems by efficient secretaries who shield them, by enclosed rooms that shut them away from day-to-day irritation, by being on the side of the building where the air-conditioning works best, by being so senior that their complaints are dealt with. However, having absorbed the ideas in this book, you know the sort of building you should be in, and you are not; and you know whether you are making the best use of the one that you have, and you are not. So you're planning to move or radically alter your building. Now is the time that you really need help.

As organizations develop, whether they grow or shrink, their needs change. Buildings are rarely exactly right for an organization for very long, if at all. Growth often involves piecemeal additions, in nearby buildings or on other floors of a larger building. This has the effect of fragmenting the organization, often just at the moment when it most needs to feel coherent. As organizations age they change their composition and way of working. Specialist skills that were initially bought in may be needed in house. Sometimes activities need special facilities, like research departments. Mergers and acquisitions create new companies, and usually these need new homes. Growth may mean that administration and communications departments become larger. Organizations also shrink and wish to surrender unnecessary space. They spin off functions into autonomous business with their own small premises. They may buy in services from other organizations rather than retain them in-house. They may have a bad year and simply lay off staff. Outside influences are also important: leases expire, market structures change, buildings become obsolete and cease to meet requirements or are even damaged in some disaster. Many scenarios occur.

Organizational changes are unlikely to fit the ad hoc building changes that are made in response to new pressures. The time comes when a radical restructuring of space is also needed. Does this mean a move? Would renovation do? Or would a simple 'scenery shift', in which partitions are moved, special rooms are refitted and new furniture is bought, be enough?

Only those responsible for implementing the mission of the company can really answer these questions, not because they will undertake and supervise the detailed decisions involved in changing buildings but because strategy and its implications are their business. They must weigh the costs and the benefits. This applies at the top, where changes affect a whole organization and its buildings, and also at the level of a department or group, where the specific changes under consideration are on a smaller scale. That is why it is vital for managers to understand some of the fundamentals about what buildings are and how office space, interior fittings and furniture interrelate. Their knowledge will help them to ask the key questions, those that will allow them to judge how far the organization's needs can, or cannot, be met in an existing building, and to assess whether proposed new layouts or buildings will perform better. A move or a renovation project is likely to be costly and disruptive, so the reasons for embarking on it must be good.

There are many examples of organizations who have misread the implications of change within and outside them and have become involved in change to their buildings that has sapped their strength just when they needed it to weather the changes around them. Recent research has found that firms that relocate at the same time as they are undergoing major restructuring are very likely to regret their move.

Many professional firms – solicitors, accountants, architects – have plunged into expensive premises in times of boom only to be forced out in subsequent recessions.

Relocation, renovation or rearrangement?

Once it is agreed that something must be done about the building, decisions are needed about precise objectives. The basic decision may be simple. Take an example. A merger has created a group of 600 people who must work together. They are currently housed too far apart for this and in several buildings, none of which has a capacity for more than 250 people. A move is essential. The choice is between a move to an existing building that will require renovation, to a newly built office that will merely need minor adaptation or to a greenfield or city site and a custom-designed building. Decisions about location in relation to image, convenience for customers and staff and costs such as rent and rates need to be taken. The relative costs of the different strategies may vary because the financial deals will depend on many factors, such as the size of the space required, the state of the property market, the location and the requirements of the organization that is moving. Each of the possible strategies may be the most suitable – none is necessarily the best; all have advantages and disadvantages.

A new, custom-designed building may give the opportunity to have precisely what you need. The process will take longer than choosing an existing building almost ready for occupation, so there must be enough time to accomplish it before you need to move. It has the advantage that staff have somewhere to work undisturbed until moving day. The opportunity may also tempt you to commission a building that you will love but that has peculiarities other organizations will not relish. Your gain as an occupier may be your loss as a property owner if your needs change in the future and new users need to be found for the building. A reality check, looking carefully at buildings occupied by other organizations, will help you to assess whether your requirements are unjustifiably unusual. This involves comparing hard facts like average lettable area per person, or space standards, proportion of enclosed space, or the amount of space given to amenities, rather than merely whether the colour scheme is attractive or the reception area has comfortable chairs, although these details are also important. There are a great many unknowns at the start of a new building project, so you need an in-house person or a team that is experienced in briefing and controlling designers, interpreting drawings and balancing conflicting requirements or is able to learn these skills in a hurry and is given the time to do so. Otherwise you must either rely on specialist advisers or take longer making decisions.

There are shades in the definition of custom design. If you commit to a speculative office development at a sufficiently early stage, it is possible to influence some aspects of the building design, such as size and number of floors or position and size of cores and entrances. It is likely that the quality and design of elements like windows, insulation and interior finishes can be specified to meet your requirements. The developers may be reluctant to go to the trouble of making changes or to deviate from the normal specification used in the buildings they market. This reluctance should not deter you from insisting at least on being told if the changes are possible, and what the extra cost will be, so that you can be a party to the decisions. If changes prove impossible, you may be able to negotiate a better financial deal on the grounds that you are being offered a standard different from the one you require.

An existing building has the advantage that you can see what you are getting. However, the more there is to see when you make your choice, the less scope there is for fundamental change. This makes it all the more important to check the basic information, reviewed in chapter 2, about sizes and efficiencies. See that it really is the size you have been told and that the design provides a high level of efficiency for the user. Consider how you will be able to make staff and clients feel good. Check the quality as well as the location of the cores. Will they allow for appropriate spaces on the office floors for your needs and sensible circulation routes without unnecessary kinks? If there are lifts, are there enough, large enough, fast enough, with large enough lobbies? Are the WCs adequate, and are those for the disabled sufficient, well located and designed in compliance with guidance? Are the service ducts accessible from the core rather than from usable space, where their opening requirements can get horribly in the way? Are there well-fitted cleaners' cupboards? Is there a sensible place for you to install an artificially ventilated smoking room?

A new developer-built building that is on the market may already be fitted out with suspended ceilings, lighting, electrical floor boxes and carpets. Estate agents often advise that this is necessary, as they believe that it will encourage tenants to lease the building if they can see what it is like when finished. Yet everyone knows that occupiers will change precisely these things to suit their needs and tastes. A vicious circle has been created, as this practice means that these items are rarely installed to a high specification, so even if you would have been happy to keep them in principle, they may simply not be good enough. A way out of this trap is provided by the concept of 'shell and core', an idea that originated in the USA. A developer provides the basic building, the shell with its cores, but no finishes or fittings and no partitions. The occupiers can then specify the required partition quality and layout and the finishes, such as carpets and ceiling tiles, and install the lighting and wiring systems that they require. In this situation there is still the need to check the sizes, efficiencies and cores and not to be carried away by the ease of implementing your fit-out and finishes so that you ignore the basic qualities, or lack of them, of the shell.

Renovation is left as the final option. This is what you do to a 'used' building, one that has been fitted out and occupied. In some cases the building may be very old; in others it may have been occupied for only a few years. The building may have been used by another organization, but renovation takes place generally when the building is occupied by the organization making the changes because of new requirements and the deterioration of the building. The difficulties of decanting the people are then added to the project. The extent of the work that you require will depend on its age and condition and how far it matches your needs. It may be necessary to strip out everything back to the 'shell and core' and start again. In some cases all that is left is the structure; the exterior 'skin' or cladding is replaced, windows are redesigned and new service cores are constructed with bigger and better lifts and ducts for air-conditioning and cable routes. Total renovation can be more expensive than a new building, so the costs must be investigated very carefully in advance. The extra may be worth paying if renovation offers things that a new building would not. For example, its location may be one in which no new buildings can be built, or it may be a historic building with unique design features. Less expense is involved in less radical renovations. A building may merely have worn out finishes, or its services, such as boilers, wiring and pipework, may need replacing, or it may need a 'scenery shift', or it may simply require redecoration throughout. Each of these is progressively less expensive, and thus, assuming that the building is suitably located, with a long enough lease on the right financial terms, that it provides enough space and that it is efficient and well designed for office uses, each is progressively more desirable.

Managing the process

Early decisions about which route to take, whether building, renovation or just some new furniture, are taken within the organization, possibly with some help and advice from outside experts. As the project progresses you need specific design and implementation skills provided either by internal staff or, more often, by independent specialists. The cast of characters in such a project can be extensive. Good management is vital and is sometimes entrusted to a project-management specialist. It is important to define carefully the roles and responsibilities of team members, including that of the project manager, and to be sure that there are no cracks through which important tasks may slip. Cost control is carried out with the help of a quantity surveyor in the UK, though this role is incorporated in the designer's role in other countries. Design may be done by a single person for a small project or by a team of design specialists with different skills for larger ones: architects for the building design, space planners who specialize in the layout of rooms and desks, interior designers for fitting out colours schemes and furniture choices, furniture designers for special products. Engineers advise on, and design, the building's structure, electrical equipment, heating, ventilation and other mechanical systems. Specialists for other requirements, from IT to landscape, from catering to audiovisual installations, can be called in. They are usually needed only if an important part of the project lies in their area of expertise. A group of users may be a formal part of the project team, with a role to play at certain points in the process. There is also a considerable number of outside organizations with which the team will interact. These include planning departments, building regulations inspectors, the utility suppliers, fire officers, insurance and security companies, all of whom will have to be consulted and their requirements met. There are numerous health and safety regulations for different activities, and standards for most products used in a building. The project team should be responsible for ensuring that regulations are adhered to and standards met. Local trade-union groups may be included in the process.

Within an organization responsibility often falls to people with little previous experience of building projects. It is important that the process is managed internally by someone who understands the business thoroughly and can therefore ensure that the building is designed or modified to serve the users' needs properly. This internal project manager is, in effect, the 'client' for the building and must be someone who has no fear about asking questions at any point in the process. A great deal of jargon is used in any specialized field, and team members must be prepared to explain, in lay terms, the decisions they are making. Ignorance is not a sign of stupidity, though failing to fill the gaps in your ignorance may be. There is a significant learning curve for people who have not familiarized themselves with how buildings behave, what happens to them over time and what users really do in them. Visits to other office buildings, talking to users about what they would have done differently if they could do it again, discussions with people who manage buildings for others, explanations by the design team of plans for other buildings with which they have been involved are all useful. Time must be allowed early on in the process to permit the learning to start, and it needs to continue throughout. The project manager must be someone who cannot be easily fobbed off with 'It's always done like this.' The reasons for doing it 'like this' must be clarified. They may be obsolete, wrong-headed, unsuitable or even non-existent. Support for the internal project manager must be given by senior management. Problems during a building project need rapid solution, otherwise deadlines are missed as critical connections in the complex pattern of events fail to be made. A director of a large organization cannot manage the process, but someone, responsible to the board, must be available if required, at least on the telephone or e-mail, even from half way around the world. Decisions have to be made about the extent to which users, the staff in general, will be consulted, how to ensure that the practical knowledge that they have is tapped, how to handle their requests, how to inform them of decisions that have been made, whether any decisions can be made 'democratically' and, if so, which. This will determine how a user group functions, how often it meets and for what purposes. Much of the success of a major building project depends on how well communication is maintained between the project team and the staff. There are several useful devices by which information can be shared even when decision making is not. One device is regular bulletins to inform all staff of the state of the project or to publicize an important decision. Presentations to all staff can be arranged to show them designs or colour schemes or to explain a critical stage that the project has reached. Information about how individuals will be affected must be supplied to them in good time, particularly the implications of decanting during the process or how the moving day will be handled. If the move is to a new location, site visits must be arranged so that people are all familiar with it before they move.

Creating the brief

The brief is the basis for decisions about what is to be built. This includes the initial decision about the available budget. In deciding performance requirements nothing should be taken for granted. A building for even fifty people should not be planned without a cleaner's cupboard. The architect who uses as his excuse 'You did not ask for one' should feel ashamed, but a full brief will help guard against obvious omissions. It may be tempting not to spend too much time on setting down the details, but unless you do, things will be forgotten. The stage at which a detailed brief is prepared for a project should include user consultation with managers and others. Those responsible for the future running and maintaining of the building should also be included in the consultation, if they are not members of the main project team. The ways in which detailed user needs and work patterns can be investigated are looked at in chapter 2. Surveys, observations, diaries and interview techniques are as valuable for briefing as they are for evaluating effects afterwards and are important ongoing management tools. It is necessary to understand the possible changes that may occur in the organization once a move is made. Trends in staff numbers and in the extent of IT use should be related to required links between groups, and a judgement should be made about how similar these will remain in the future. Knowledge of the implications of transport and the ways in which the local amenities of the area are used may affect decisions about the provisions of facilities within a new building.

Organizational policies must be considered. These concern large issues, basic to the working patterns in the organization, and small issues that equally describe its character and aspirations. Important decisions about space standards and cellularization should not merely be taken for granted. Policies and standards may have already been formulated. As often as not, they are absent, incomplete or out of date, so they need to be reconsidered.

Art or plants may seem to be more trivial issues. There may be no formal policies about them. Now is the time to formulate them. Perhaps they are to be incorporated in the scheme to impress clients or provide pleasant surroundings for staff, or perhaps the policy is not to have any. Each approach will indicate something about the organizational culture, as will a failure to have considered the issue, which will mean they are absent by default or haphazardly organized.

As usual, storage is of particular importance. Do not assume that in new premises, wonderfully organized on the most modern principles, the need for odd bits of storage will be reduced. Although new approaches to deliveries may be adopted, 'just in time' being a system as well suited to office consumables as to a manufacturing plant, these will not lead to a no-store-room scenario. Apart from all the work-associated files and storerooms, an office of 1,000 people can use sixty cases of WC rolls in four weeks. Spare parts for furniture will need to be stored, as will unwanted or broken items, equipment and the Christmas decorations. There must be a janitor's store able to accommodate housekeeping supplies and general store rooms for other items. Basements and attics may not exist or may not be designed to accommodate such things.

The staff user group can continue to provide useful ongoing input for the professional design team as the design develops. Its members should have an opportunity to examine and comment on designs at several stages. These stages, and the nature of the process, should be set out early on, so that everyone is clear what the proposed pattern of consultation will be, and no false expectations are raised. Many decisions cannot be left to this group. The precise scope of staff decisions needs to be made clear and may relate more to details than to major decisions about purchases. A furniture range, for example, may be agreed on by the main project team while allowing the staff group to select the colour and fabrics for carpets and chairs, or one of a narrow range of furniture options may be selected through user input, while the colour scheme is fixed whatever the range selected. Where possible, a mock-up of the proposed furniture, or an opportunity for representatives of the users to visit an office using that furniture, should be arranged, so that details of comfort and function can be checked. Users are a valuable resource, and their opinions should be used to achieve the best possible arrangement of furniture and equipment. One point at which the user group can make a valuable contribution is at an early stage in the layout planning, since they are familiar with the details of work patterns and processes. Even when radical, possibly unpopular, changes may be suggested, what staff say about the existing system has relevance, and is of use to, the design team, but in these circumstances users must not be led to believe that the new processes will be abandoned just because they believe the old ones are better.

Too many changes rock the ark

> *'The office is too far out of town. It is isolated, making lunchtime a bore.'*
>
> *'Now too far away from town for personal activities, re bank, etc.'*
>
> *'Location is very inconvenient – no shops, banks, facilities nearby. A poor choice of site for a major organization. Right on the very edge of the city, one is totally dependent on a car.'*
>
> Questionnaire responses: clerical workers after an office move to town fringe

The disruptions caused to staff by a move are well explored in management literature. Relocation and the effects on 'human resources' have long been a subject of concern. The problems are real and need to be taken seriously. When a journey to work is lengthened, or the transport mode shifts, or a new location involves moving house, the web of family life patterns, developed and adapted to fit the old situation, has to be changed. Help may be needed by some people; sympathy is required all round. There are other ways in which a move may cause disruption. People react to their office with strong feelings. If they have other reasons for discontent, then the building may have enough imperfections to act as a focus for their feelings of frustration or dislocation.

A new or renovated building is a new opportunity. If the need for a change in premises results from organizational restructuring, everyone needs to adapt and create new working relationships. This takes time. While moving to a new building may seem an ideal opportunity to replace out-of-date systems, such as telephone exchanges or computer networks, beware of undertaking too many changes simultaneously. Systems that do not perform as expected, in a new place, with a new group of people striving to fulfil a restructured mission, can be crippling. Planning a new office automation system is worth while; providing the necessary cable networks and locations for central equipment in the new building, so that the change can take place smoothly at a later date, is prudent. Funds for the purchase can be allocated and incorporated in the planned budget for the new building. A new system, with its inevitable teething troubles, may be best introduced several months in advance of the move, or left for a few months until the organization feels like a working entity rather than an amalgam of disparate parts. Whether this is an appropriate stance depends on a number of factors. How bad is the existing system? How incompatible are systems that must be brought together? How radical are the organizational changes that are taking place? Will it save serious future disruption to make the changes immediately? These are all questions that must be considered.

Whatever decision is taken, one objective of a project should be, as argued throughout this book, to ensure that future changes can be made. The building that you move into on hand-over day is not a fixed, perfect solution. Easily accessible and adaptable routes for cables will ensure that any system can be replaced with minimum disruption as it becomes out of date. Careful choice of locations for installations that will be hard to move later will ensure that the building can adapt and provide a good home for a changing business over a long lifetime.

Moving day

The move itself must be carefully orchestrated. Moving 2,000 people is far more complicated than moving twenty, but, whatever the scale of the task, the same principles apply. They apply to the decant-and-reoccupy activities that are as much a part of renovation as of a whole-sale move. The overriding requirement is that a move should not disrupt the work of the organization. To this end careful, systematic planning of the actual move must be undertaken. Someone must be responsible for the process and see that everyone plays their part. One person's time (or a team's time for a monster move) spent in advance is better value than everyone's frustration on the day. Some points to watch:

- Plan ahead – work to a written plan, with as much help as you need. There are firms that specialize in move planning if you have insufficient in-house resources to cope.
- Provide clear labels for people to use on their boxes and belongings, and full instructions on what they are expected to do in advance and on move day.
- If the move has to take place in stages (for example, over several weekends) set up a rhythm so that a fixed sequence of activities takes place regularly each week for each group as it prepares to move.
- Concentrate on storage, and do so well in advance. Destroy anything redundant. Archive anything not actively needed. Offer incentives to people to get rid of as much as possible. See to it that new workplaces are equipped with suitable, sufficient storage but not overprovided.

- Saving overtime costs by removal men working only on weekdays may be a false economy as it usually means the loss of several working days.
- On move days provide sandwiches at lunch for the removal teams so they don't disappear off site for hours.
- Aim to keep the piles of crates and boxes in the new space stacked well below eye level. There's nothing more depressing than moving into a new office, aiming to start work promptly and efficiently and feeling you are struggling through a confusing and impenetrable maze of rubbish.
- Give everyone in the new building a 'welcome pack' of information about how the building works and what to do if it doesn't, what shops and services are available near by and where groups are located within the building. A loose-leaf version, which can take additional pages as new issues come to the fore, is a good idea, incorporated in a binder with other useful material, like diary pages or a year planner. A message saying 'Welcome' on everyone's computer screen helps establish the positive aspects of the move.

Facilities management

The facilities-management role is another story. It starts at this point and, well executed, will contribute to the benefits you can expect from your building. The appearance of the office can have a powerful effect on the morale of staff and the opinion of visitors. It will depend on the way that the office is designed in the first place and on the entire approach to its management during use. 'Facilities management' is the term used to describe the amalgam of roles involved in ensuring that a building operates at its best in relation to the needs of the users. It covers a wide range of tasks: space management, building and services maintenance and repair, furniture and equipment repair or disposal, the preparation of telephone directories, cleaning, office supplies, maintaining a tidy office, the management of energy, security and other policies, booking routines for facilities, catering, looking after plants.

Each task should have targets. The effectiveness of the activities carried out should be monitored so that remedial action can be taken if standards are not met. This may be carried out by internal or outside teams. To carry it out effectively requires the systematic collection and use of a considerable range of information. First and foremost, the completion of a move is the ideal moment to update all information. The project team can be asked, as part of their role or contract, to provide this service at the end of the job. Necessary information that should be available from the team includes up-to-date plans of building and plant installations, desk and services layouts, a furniture and equipment inventory, operating manuals, maintenance information, addresses of suppliers and regulatory bodies, certificates of compliance, directory of staff locations, telephone extensions and e-mail addresses. This information must be regularly updated and safely stored. Training in its use may be needed. Other information resides within the organization and must be accumulated over time. This includes a current organizational chart and space allocations, cost information about services, maintenance, cleaning and other contracts, a planned maintenance schedule and the state of play at any time. The challenge of keeping the building tuned and responsive has begun.

Post-occupancy evaluation

As with all management decisions, you cannot be sure your offices do what they should unless you find out. After the moving dust has settled, you need to discover what works and what does not. You can do this by informal walkabouts, looking for untoward changes that people have made, chatting to them, specifically asking departments for feedback, or by commissioning full surveys from specialists. Just as your new car has its first inspection after the first few thousand miles, so your new building needs an initial inspection and another after several months. Regular checks are also needed, akin to the MOT. Knowing what the niggles are means that adjustments can be made. Rearrangements will start almost before everyone has settled down. Your organization may need to make another office move soon. Make sure that feedback helps to refine every aspect of the next move, wherever it takes place.

Now enjoy your building

You have worked hard to get to this point. Despite any setbacks and imperfections, you have a better building than before. The move should be an occasion to celebrate. You have worked out what you need, and, with a few compromises, you have succeeded in getting it. The building can continue to be a pleasure to use, a productive environment for staff as well as being serviceable and cost-effective, for many years. Your ark is ready to sail, with all aboard, towards a productive future.

Summary

This chapter gives you guidance in deciding whether you need to make a major move and, if so, how to go about it.

Organizational needs change for many reasons, and some demand a change in the office building. A choice between relocation, renovation and rearrangement is the first step in the process. Each has advantages and disadvantages. The most radical is relocation to another building. It may be new, custom-built or speculative. A new building can exactly fit your needs but may take a long time to construct and equip and is hard to visualize before you start. An existing one can be cheaper and quicker to occupy but may not meet your requirements as well. If a great deal has to be renovated, it can cost more than a new building. Sometimes an appropriate 'scenery shift' may be all you need.

The process involves teamwork by management, staff and outside experts. There is an important role for the internal project manager, who must be determined, patient and persistent. Learning by visiting other buildings is important, particularly if the manager has little previous experience of relocation projects.

The written brief contains the instructions from the client to all the team. It is a reference point and should be written down. It may need to go into considerable detail. It should be based on organizational policies and can offer an opportunity to clarify these if they have not hitherto been formalized. There is a role for staff input, but how extensive must be made clear at the outset. There may not be many decisions that can be taken democratically, other than the finishing touches of local colours, choice of art or placing of plants, but users' experience is needed to design work layouts that will function well.

A move is a disruptive period. It is inadvisable to use this time for the complete reorganization of multiple aspects of the business. Some additional alterations may have to take place after occupation. This underlines one of the important arguments in this book, that changes will continue to happen throughout the life of any building. Changes in the plan, layout and services, to accommodate new needs and replace ageing elements, must be allowed for so that they are easy to make.

A well-planned move is one that is planned in advance. A systematic approach that takes care of details is vital. Storage must be sorted out rigorously. Staff will feel good if the environment is kept tidy during the move and information that they need is available. After the move the management of the building will be greatly helped by having clear information, some of which should be obtained from the design team as part of the contract with them.

A good project is an occasion to celebrate. Whether new or refurbished, a new office environment should be enjoyed by staff and can help your company to be more productive.

Further Reading

Bailey, S., *Offices*, Butterworth Architecture, London, 1990

Becker, F., *The Changing Facilities Organization*, Project Office Furniture plc, London, 1988

Becker, F., *The Total Workplace: Facilities Management and the Elastic Organization*, Van Nostrand Reinhold, New York, 1990

Berger-Levrault, *L'Empire du bureau 1900–2000*, Berger-Levrault, Nancy, 1984

Bordass, W., and Leaman, A., 'User and Occupant Controls in Office Buildings' in E. Sterling, C. Bieva and C. Collet (eds.), *Building Design, Technology and Occupant Well-being in Temperate Climates: Conference Proceedings*, ASHRAE, Atlanta, 1993

Brandt, P., *Office Design*, Whitney Library of Design, New York, 1992

Brill, M., *et al.* and Buffalo Organization for Social and Technological Innovation, *Using Office Space to Increase Productivity*, BOSTI, Buffalo, 1984

Brill, M., *Now Offices, No Offices, New Offices: Wild Times in the World of Office Work*, Tekmon, Toronto, 1994

British Council for Offices, *Specification for Urban Offices*, Reading, 1994

Building Research Establishment BREEAM/New Offices, *An Environmental Assessment for New Office Designs*, BRE Publications, Watford, 1993

Clarke, A. C., *Profiles of the Future*, Gollancz, London, 1962; 2nd edn, Pan, London, 1973

Craig, M., *Office Workers' Survival Handbook: A Guide to Fighting Health Hazards in the Office*, BSSRS, London, 1981

Curwell, C., March, C., and Venables, R. (eds.), *Buildings and Health: The Rosehaugh Guide*, RIBA Publications, London, 1990

Duffy, F., Cave, C., and Worthington, J., *Planning Office Space*, The Architectural Press, London, 1976

Duffy, F., and Henney, A., *The Changing City*, Bulstrode Press, London, 1990

Duffy, F., *The Changing Workplace*, Phaidon, London, 1992

Duffy, F., Laing, A., and Crisp, V., *The Responsible Workplace*, Butterworth Architecture and Estates Gazette, London, 1993

Eley, J., 'Intelligent Buildings', *Facilities*, vol. 4, no. 4, April 1986, pp. 4–10

Eley, J., 'The Green Office: Policy and Practice', *Facilities*, vol. 7, no. 5, May 1989, pp. 16–17

Eley, J., 'Lines of Enquiry', *Premises and Facilities Management*, June 1993, pp. 37–40

Eley, J., 'Office and Laboratory Furniture', *Specification*, EMAP, London, 1993

Gorman, F., and Brown, C. (eds.), *The Responsive Office*, Steelcase Strafor/Polymath Publishing, Streatley-on-Thames, 1990

Handy, C., *The Empty Raincoat*, Hutchinson, London, 1994

Harris, D. A., *et al.*, *Planning and Designing the Office Environment*, Van Nostrand Reinhold, New York, 1991

Hartkopf, V., *et al.*, *Designing the Office of the Future: The Japanese Approach to Tomorrow's Workplace*, John Wiley and Sons, New York, 1993

Health and Safety Commission, *Workplace (Health, Safety and Welfare) Regulations*, HMSO, London, 1992

Hillier, W., and Hanson, J., *Social Logic of Space*, Cambridge University Press, Cambridge, 1984

Kleeman, W. B., Jr, *Interior Design in the Electronic Office: The Comfort and Productivity Payoff*, Van Nostrand Reinhold, New York, 1991

Knobel, L., *Office Furniture*, Unwin Hyman, London, 1987.

Laing, A., 'The Shrinking HQ: Can Cost Cutting Allow for Innovation?', *Facilities*, vol. 8, no. 8, August 1990, pp. 17–20

Laing, A., 'Desk Sharing: The Politics of Space', *Facilities*, vol. 8, no. 7, July 1990, pp. 12–19

Leaman, A., 'Designing for Manageability', *Building Services*, March 1993

Leaman, A., 'Discomfort and Complexity', *Architects' Journal*, October 1993.

Lloyd, B., *Offices and Office Work: The Coming Revolution*, Staniland Hall, London, 1990

Marberry S., *Color in the Office*, Van Nostrand Reinhold, New York, 1994.

Marmot, A. F., 'Flexible Work', *Facilities*, vol. 10, no. 11, November 1992, pp. 20–22

Marmot, A. F., 'Managing Empty Space' *Facilities*, vol. 10, no. 9, September 1992, p. 6

Marmot, A. F., 'The Good Office: Post-occupancy Evaluation of Office Buildings', *Facilities*, vol. 9, no. 12, December 1991, pp. 10–13

Marmot, A. F., '"Just in Time" Office Space', *Director*, June 1991, p. 99

Marmot, A. F., 'Control of Smoking in the Workplace', *Facilities*, vol. 8, no. 4, April 1990, pp. 8–11

Mole, J., *Brits at Work*, Brealey, London, 1992

Rappoport, J. E., Cushman, R. F., and Daroff, K. (eds.), *Office Planning and Design: Desk Reference*, John Wiley and Sons, New York, 1992

Rayfield, J. K., *The Office Interior Design Guide*, John Wiley and Sons, New York, 1994

Steele, F., 'The Ecology of Executive Teams: A New View of the Top', *Organizational Dynamics* (American Management Association), Spring 1983, pp. 65–78

Stansall, P., 'Planning Government Buildings', *The Architects' Journal*, 18 May 1994

Sundstrom, E., *Workplaces: The Psychology of the Physical Environment in Offices and Factories*, Cambridge University Press, Cambridge, 1986

Toffler, A., *Powershift*, Bantam, London, 1991

Tutt, P., and Adler, D., *New Metric Handbook: Planning and Design Data*, Butterworth Architecture, London, 1979

Vischer, J., *Environmental Quality in Offices*, Van Nostrand Reinhold, New York, 1989

White, J. R. (ed.), *The Office Building: From Concept to Investment Reality*, Counselors of Real Estate, Chicago, 1993

Williams, B., *Facilities Economics*, Building Economics Bureau, Bromley, 1995

Wilson, A., *Are You Sitting Comfortably?*, Optima Books, London, 1994

Wilson, S., *Premises of Excellence: How Successful Companies Manage Their Offices*, Herman Miller, London, 1985

Wineman, J. D. (ed.), *Behavioural Issues in Office Design*, Van Nostrand Reinhold, New York, 1986

Index

READ MORE IN PENGUIN

In every corner of the world, on every subject under the sun, Penguin represents quality and variety – the very best in publishing today.

For complete information about books available from Penguin – including Puffins, Penguin Classics and Arkana – and how to order them, write to us at the appropriate address below. Please note that for copyright reasons the selection of books varies from country to country.

In the United Kingdom: Please write to *Dept. JC, Penguin Books Ltd, FREEPOST, West Drayton, Middlesex UB7 0BR.*

If you have any difficulty in obtaining a title, please send your order with the correct money, plus ten per cent for postage and packaging, to *PO Box No. 11, West Drayton, Middlesex UB7 0BR*

In the United States: Please write to *Consumer Sales, Penguin USA, P.O. Box 999, Dept. 17109, Bergenfield, New Jersey 07621-0120.* VISA and MasterCard holders call 1-800-253-6476 to order all Penguin titles

In Canada: Please write to *Penguin Books Canada Ltd, 10 Alcorn Avenue, Suite 300, Toronto, Ontario M4V 3B2*

In Australia: Please write to *Penguin Books Australia Ltd, P.O. Box 257, Ringwood, Victoria 3134*

In New Zealand: Please write to *Penguin Books (NZ) Ltd, Private Bag 102902, North Shore Mail Centre, Auckland 10*

In India: Please write to *Penguin Books India Pvt Ltd, 706 Eros Apartments, 56 Nehru Place, New Delhi 110 019*

In the Netherlands: Please write to *Penguin Books Netherlands bv, Postbus 3507, NL-1001 AH Amsterdam*

In Germany: Please write to *Penguin Books Deutschland GmbH, Metzlerstrasse 26, 60594 Frankfurt am Main*

In Spain: Please write to *Penguin Books S. A., Bravo Murillo 19, 1° B, 28015 Madrid*

In Italy: Please write to *Penguin Italia s.r.l., Via Felice Casati 20, I–20124 Milano*

In France: Please write to *Penguin France S. A., 17 rue Lejeune, F–31000 Toulouse*

In Japan: Please write to *Penguin Books Japan, Ishikiribashi Building, 2–5–4, Suido, Bunkyo-ku, Tokyo 112*

In Greece: Please write to *Penguin Hellas Ltd, Dimocritou 3, GR–106 71 Athens*

In South Africa: Please write to *Longman Penguin Southern Africa (Pty) Ltd, Private Bag X08, Bertsham 2013*

READ MORE IN PENGUIN

BUSINESS AND ECONOMICS

North and South David Smith

'This authoritative study ... gives a very effective account of the incredible centralization of decision-making in London, not just in government and administration, but in the press, communications and the management of every major company' – *New Statesman & Society*

I am Right – You are Wrong Edward de Bono

Edward de Bono expects his ideas to outrage conventional thinkers, yet time has been on his side, and the ideas that he first put forward twenty years ago are now accepted mainstream thinking. Here, in this brilliantly argued assault on outmoded thought patterns, he calls for nothing less than a New Renaissance.

Lloyds Bank Small Business Guide Sara Williams

This long-running guide to making a success of your small business deals with real issues in a practical way. 'As comprehensive an introduction to setting up a business as anyone could need' – *Daily Telegraph*

The *Economist* Economics Rupert Pennant-Rea and Clive Crook

Based on a series of 'briefs' published in the *Economist* , this is a clear and accessible guide to the key issues of today's economics for the general reader.

The Rise and Fall of Monetarism David Smith

Now that even Conservatives have consigned monetarism to the scrap heap of history, David Smith draws out the unhappy lessons of a fundamentally flawed economic experiment, driven by a doctrine that for years had been regarded as outmoded and irrelevant.

Understanding Organizations Charles B. Handy

Of practical as well as theoretical interest, this book shows how general concepts can help solve specific organizational problems.